FOSTER DOGGIE
INSANITY

Tips & Tales to Keep your Kool as a Doggie Foster Parent

TAMIRA CI THAYNE D.N.

WHO chains YOU
PUBLISHING

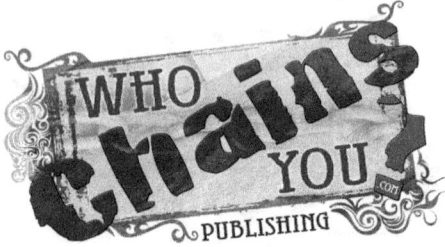

Published by Who Chains You Publishing
P.O. Box 581
Amissville, VA 20106

www.TamiraThayne.com
www.WhoChainsYou.com

Author photo by Brynakha Vaettir

ISBN: 978-0-9842897-8-3

Printed in the United States of America

First Edition

TO THOSE I MOST CHERISH:
JOE, RAYNE, AND BRYN

AND THE CHAINED DOGS I'VE LOVED AND LOST:
BO, ROSIE, SESS, SADIE, MAGNUM,
BANSHEE, AND SLOAN

WHAT DOGGIE FOSTER PARENTS HAVE SAID ABOUT
this Book's 1st Edition, "Scream Like Banshee"

&

"I regularly buy books with a rescue theme but always felt a bit disappointed because there hasn't been a book that portrayed my rescue experiences. So I wasn't really prepared for Tamira Ci Thayne's *Scream Like Banshee*. It is the most honest account of the perils and pitfalls as well as the joy and fulfillment that rescue volunteers face daily. The book was beautifully written and brutally honest...Thayne's book feels like an embrace from a friend that understands what we all go through. It is a beacon of hope to let other rescuers know that they are not alone. It is a must read for anyone involved in rescue."—Amy Snyder, Volunteer for Dachshund Rescue of North America

"I have been doing rescue for years. When I started to read *Scream Like Banshee*, it was like reading my own story. I never thought that it would be so similar to the way I did rescue, but it was as if I had written the book myself. I recommend it to anyone who does rescue or fostering. It helps to know that you are not the only one that feels a certain way at a certain time. I also recommend it to anyone who is thinking of helping dogs in need. It will prepare you for what is to come in your life. GREAT BOOK!" —Joe Maringo, SPARRO.org

"I loved every single minute of it! I couldn't put it down. I've been in animal rescue since 2000 and am currently with a rescue group which pulls animals from high-kill animal shelters and home-fosters them after getting them vetted. Thayne's book spoke volumes to me. I so appreciate her sense of humor and her ability to say just exactly what needs to be said."—Carol Schmidt, Missouri

"Whether you've fostered hundreds of dogs or none, it is an enjoyable read, mixing laughter and empathy with real life situations. Thayne may even leave you questioning everything you thought you knew about our canine companions and the people who care about them. A book that is more than a tool for fostering; it is a declaration of the spirit, heart and soul of Dogs Deserve Better, its founder and rescuers universally. The moral to this story is 'It's OK not to be perfect; a dog will love you anyway.'"—Dawn Ashby, former Dogs Deserve Better rep

"I just read *Scream Like Banshee* and I can't say how much I LOVED it! I've been fostering for nearly four years, over 120 dogs, and your book was everything I needed to hear. At one time two years ago I had 19 dogs. Never again! I definitely learned from my mistakes but I have beat myself up over some of them. Living without the guilt and moving on is what I got from the book, and what I needed to hear. I'm down to two and just took my first vacation in 6 years. Thank you, Thank you, Thank you!"—Cathy Sullivan, Oklahoma

ALSO BY AUTHOR TAMIRA THAYNE

℘

Rescue Smiles: Favorite Animal Stories
of Love and Liberation

More Rescue Smiles: Best-Loved
Animal Tales of Resilience and Redemption

Capitol in Chains:
54 Days of the Doghouse Blues

Unchain My Heart: Dogs Deserve Better
Rescue Stories of Courage and Compassion

The Chained Gods Series
(The Wrath of Dog, The King's Tether,
The Knight's Chain, and The Curse of Cur)

Smidgey Pidgey's Predicament
(The Animal Protectors Series Vol. 1)

Spittin' Kitten's Speed-Away
(The Animal Protectors Series Vol. 2)

Happy Dog! Coloring Book:
From Chained to Cherished

PREFACE

❧

The image you see on the cover of this book is a stock photo image. It's a staged shot, not 'real' life, and I love it. Why? Because it's how I wish doggie foster parenting could be—I'd walk my tiny foster doggie down the street, her red leash matching my designer pumps, my couture dress swaying with each sexy stride. (What? Why have a daydream if you're not sexy in it?) And then once in awhile, oops, Princess and I'd get tangled in the leash. *Goodness Gracious!* But soon we're back in sync again, swishing our way up the block, being envied by all those who wish they were as cute a couple as we are.

Ah! We *are* a vision of loveliness...*but who am I kidding.* My reality couldn't be any more different, even without the foster doggie added into the mix. No doggie foster parent I've met routinely dresses and acts like the girl on the cover, but I believe it's not out of the realm of possibility; in fact, I'd like to invite those folks, if they do exist, to join our foster brigade. I'm sure a group local to you could find an easy foster (contrary to popular belief, they aren't as rare as unicorns) that wouldn't soil your attire, and maybe this dream of mine and the picture on the cover could mesh to become a reality.

In my experience, fostering is not for wimps, cowards, or the otherwise mess-or-insanity-challenged. Doggie foster parents who make it look easy are either living the sweet life

I call denial, or they are the Mother Theresa of Doggieland.

I am neither of these.

This book is an updated version of 2008's *Scream Like Banshee: 29 Days of Tips and Tales to Save your Sanity as a Doggie Foster Parent,* which was named after my foster dog Banshee, a black lab who was majorly talented at crazy-making, and forced me to take a good look at myself.

Crates ripped asunder, fences demolished, couches obliterated, doors splintered...these are the nightmares that routinely go along with doggie fostering, and Banshee boy could do them all in spades.

Granted, caring for a dog with issues may—with an emphasis on the may—still be easier than fostering a human child, but some days you might just be tempted to trade in for the human.

I've come to notice during my fourteen plus years of fostering dogs that the dogs aren't the only ones who could use a teensy bit of help. *Those of us helping the dogs could use a leg up ourselves.*

The animal advocacy community has its share of issues—a large slice of the issue pie in my opinion—but there's a dichotomy I've noticed amongst dog advocates that really gets my goat: we have those who—although they crosspost all day long and wonder why the infamous 'they' aren't stepping up to take a dog in need—never seem to feel an urge to do the dirty deed themselves.

Then we have those who—in a saintly but just as disturbingly unhealthy pattern—feel the overwhelming need to take in every abused dog that crosses their never-turned-off computer screens.

It's usually the first group, the Never-Get-Their-Hands-Dirtiers, who claim the second group is not doing enough because such-and-such dog is still in need of a foster home. At which point, in an effort to save their reputation, the Saints-of-Self-Sacrifice feel they must do more, even though they already have 22 dogs and a major outbreak of kennel cough. These folks rush out to find a coupla' hard cases to drag home in order to appease group #1 and somehow feel all is right in their world again.

This book is for you guys. All of you.

We've got to find the balance, and somehow the idea of balance, as it applies to fostering dogs, has bypassed our movement.

It is my goal to bring us, as a group, back to the middle—the gray area—where the deer and the foster dogs play.

Where those who can't foster because their-mother-lives-in-Alaska-and-she-may-come-to-visit-within-the-next-two-years-at-which-point-the-dog-might-cause-a-run-in-her-$50-stockings step up and do just a little, and those who cry-themselves-to-sleep-every-night-at-3-a.m.-after-tak-ing-care-of-15-dogs-drinking-a-bottle-of-wine-and-eating-27-twinkies step back and realize they have to start taking care of themselves, too.

After we each give a little, we can all live happily ever af-ter in our perfect world, with our perfect dogs, in our perfect mansions, overlooking the rolling hills of our own little per-fect doggie heaven.

Ah, now doesn't that feel better? Let's do this!

INTRODUCTION

ℰ

Banshee with his ball after swimming in the river.

This book and its predecessor, *Scream Like Banshee*, were inspired by my real life experiences in doggie fostering—ones I wouldn't trade but also wouldn't wish on anyone—and my subsequent trip through and out the other side of Hades. My foster dog Banshee was so psychologically damaged from his life on the chain that his pain became my pain, and the struggle we both faced to come to a place of understanding and positivity is burned into my psyche.

I heard you Banshee. I just didn't know how to help you.

❧

Before I started Dogs Deserve Better in 2002, I didn't even know that people fostered dogs just like they foster children—except for less pay and greater rewards. Today I know there are thousands of us out there, people just like me who've undergone the ups and downs of helping homeless dogs so they don't die in shelters or at the end of a chain.

I know it's hard. Having fostered over 250 dogs myself, I offer these tips for those of you who struggle with the difficult task, and feel like you're just not cut out for it. I hope to make fostering easier for you so you can be easier on yourself.

I also offer these tips for those of you who haven't yet dipped your toes in the foster-parent pool. I encourage you to just do it.

This is not a book about dog training, but a book about people training while working with dogs, so you can learn to manage your expectations, cut your workload, and keep your kool while fostering.

I wish I could claim to be the perfect doggie foster parent, but, even after all this time, nope, I'm still not. Some days my patience is shredded and I'm driven to the brink of insanity by whatever new foster is pushing my buttons. I've made the journey from crazy foster parent to calm (ok, calmer) family lead over a period of thirteen years, and sometimes it still feels like I have a ways to go. But I'm not stopping now, and neither are you if you're on this journey with me.

I retired from my position as CEO of Dogs Deserve Better in March of 2015, ending a 13-year period of extremely active doggie foster-parenting. I made a vow to myself—and to the dogs—that I would foster at least one dog per year for as long as I'm physically able, because I know the need is great.

I'm now firmly in that middle ground where many of you are or long to be, with the ability to do SOMETHING even when I'm no longer leading an active national rescue organization. This winter I lived up to my promise, fostering two dogs who you'll meet further into the book, and finding them a loving home and family, together. I will continue to do so yearly, and I hope you'll join me in this pledge.

When I talk about my adventures in dog rescue and what I have gone through to foster and advocate on behalf of chained dogs, my family and friends are usually dumbfounded. They don't know why I would put myself through it; sometimes I didn't either.

It certainly wasn't for the pay.

It certainly wasn't for the recognition.

It certainly wasn't for the (un)popularity contest.

It was for them.

These dogs.

They got to me.

And I was and still am driven to make a difference in their lives.

If you don't know me or Dogs Deserve Better, welcome to a brief look into what was my daily life with fostered, formerly-chained dogs, and the lessons I learned from interacting with them. I hope to open your eyes to the pleading in theirs, and the necessity of opening our homes and hearts to a foster dog in need.

I aim to give you simple, daily tips for keeping your sanity while fostering. You are not alone in your struggles, and you are not the first to feel you can't press on. We can press on together.

Worthless, in his 'improved location' after my complaints...even more mud.

I began devoting myself to chained dogs in 2002, after suffering six-years in the bastions of Hell watching a chained black Labrador retriever named Worthless pace day in and day out—chained to a wooden post—1/4 mile from my home. He was often so tangled around both the post and a nearby tree that he couldn't reach his house or any shelter from the elements.

Only God knows how many nights he spent shivering, huddled in the cold and mud, unable to get himself to safety because he was shackled with a formerly 10-foot chain which had somehow become a 2-foot noose.

I felt so helpless and so hopeless watching him suffer that I was driven to do something about it. I discovered that current laws were on the side of abusers, and looking to local authorities for help got me nowhere.

I formed Dogs Deserve Better, a non-profit organization which advocated exclusively for America's chained, penned, and backyard dogs, and launched myself into the adventure of a lifetime.

By the time I left Dogs Deserve Better I had lived with, fostered, and trained over 250 dogs that came from nothing, and had no idea how to live inside the home with the family. When I started I was so young (at 39!) and naive, and knew nothing of what I was getting myself into.

This is my story, well, 30 days of it anyway, with daily tips for you as a foster parent, and tales of foster parenting gone right or gone wrong. This is Banshee's story, the story of what he taught me, and the story of his foster siblings.

If you too struggle at times as a doggie foster parent, my hope is that this book will bring you solace and ideas for self-care while fostering. There is no shame in not being 'the perfect foster parent.' Such a thing doesn't exist.

Animal rescuers can and often do suffer immense psychological distress, up to and including Compassion Fatigue Syndrome, i.e. burnout. Remember, your emotional and physical health needs to be a priority, too. Welcome.

Chapter 1

Dogs Need Foster Homes: Yes, Even You Can Foster

ɤ

A beagle I photographed, networked, and transported to her new, inside home and family. Now she goes for spa visits! Get involved.

Truth: Six million chained and penned dogs waiting for freedom—as well as other homeless and rejected companions of all breeds and sizes in shelters and rescue groups—need a soft place to land while they understand what went wrong and how to be the kind of companion humans need and want.

Tip: If you've never fostered before, foster one—until there are none.

Repeat after me: I too can foster, I too can foster, I CAN and WILL foster!

Definition: Fostering (as it applies to dogs) is taking a dog into your home until he/she is adopted out to a new and wonderful home and family. This includes: allowing the dog access to the same amenities as your own companions; ensuring vet care and housetraining are provided either by you or the rescue group through which you foster; and, teaching them to live with a family so that they will be: 1. more adoptable, 2. happier, and 3. not returned from their shiny new, inside homes and families.

I want every one of you to foster a dog; let me be right up front about that. You are needed. Maybe you don't have a really good idea how great the need is.

Let me explain—the need is great.

When I was with DDB (Dogs Deserve Better) I was asked every single day by someone, somewhere, to take in a dog. A dog that was suffering. A dog that needed help. And every single day I had to turn someone away, some dog that was suffering, some dog that needed help.

We have the power to stop this madness; we as a collective whole, as a group of dog lovers, are a group of people who can make a serious, serious difference.

Note: Much of the foster diary you'll read on these pages tells Banshee's story, and that of his foster brothers and sisters, in order to illustrate for you the joys and sorrows of rescue. Although this comes was from a particular time frame in my rescue career, it bears similarities to other rescuers plights, and in reality could be any of our stories at any time in our lives.

Foster Diary: Just as I'm wrapping up the daily e-mails and starting on my backlog of DDB tasks (who knew running a nonprofit would be so much work), a local Bellwood, Pennsylvania guy calls me about a malamute in a pen at the back of his neighbor's apartment. He tells me she has a tumor on her back, her hair is falling out, she's skinny, and she never has food or water.

Most of the phone calls DDB gets are about out-of-state dogs, so it's not something I can personally act on; I usually give advice or pass them along to a local DDB area rep. When a call comes in about one near me I can't help but get excited about the possibility of freeing the dog, and feel compelled to act quickly.

I especially enjoy it when the caller is a guy, because in general guys are much more mind-your-own-business-y than women, and it gives me hope for the evolution of mankind. He explains to me that he has tried to ignore the poor dog's plight, but he is afraid she isn't going to make it through the winter.

He's been putting water and food into her pen during the day when the caretakers aren't home. He also tells me it's an apartment building, and the owner of the building—

although not a dog lover—is not too happy about the dog being outside either.

I see possibilities in that tidbit of information, and I tell
him he needs to really work that angle. If he's a good tenant,
the landlord will be inclined to take steps to ensure that he
remains happy, and tell the other tenants that the dog can't
stay outside.

Since the dog's caretakers are not home, and they aren't
the owners of the property, I grab my camera and drive over
to take pics with little fear of trespassing. The neighbor will
walk me back to meet the dog and show me the conditions.

I had thought I knew all the chained and penned dogs in
Bellwood—it's a small town—and to think there's one that
hasn't gotten our information yet chaps me.

As is often the case, the dog isn't in quite the dire shape
he's described; people tend to exaggerate when they are telling me about the conditions to make sure I'll help. What they
don't realize is that any chained/penned dog is in need of

help just by virtue of living ostracized, so there's no need to convince me that their conditions are unacceptable!

I see right away that what he thinks is loss of fur is actually just blowing coat, normal for breeds like huskies, akitas, and malamutes. The malamute does indeed have a tumor on her back, which I hope will motivate the humane officer to insist they take her to the vet. She is also a bit underweight, and he says she NEVER has water when he visits with her.

She's a beautiful girl, and sweet as can be, with one blue eye and one brown eye. I fall for her easily, and feel so badly for her stuck out here with no human interaction and no love.

I leave the caretakers a doorhanger, brochure, and a newsletter. Upon returning home I immediately call and leave a message for the humane officer (Officer G.) with the address, description of the dog, and a request for him to make a visit.

To say I don't like this officer would be an understatement. He's got territory issues (a trait shared by many humane and animal control officers), and he's warned me from Day One to stay off his turf—under the guise of keeping me safe, of course—so very kind of him.

This is the very same officer who left me holding the bag on a dying shepherd named Doogie, who was unable to stand for three days after being chained for years. When the officer failed to respond to calls for help from the neighbors, they begged me to do something for the dog.

I made no promises, but drove to the address, where I saw that the reported condition of the dog was not exaggerated. I thought he was dead at first! My assistant and I documented the situation with photos and video, and then picked up the dog and drove him to the vet. To do otherwise would have been the real criminal act. Officer G. met me at the vet, carried the dog inside, and then told me he would go get a warrant for the dog. He lied.

Instead, he told the police I had taken the dog; when I refused to return the dog to the loving folks who left him there to die, I was arrested and dragged through the court system. I sent Doogie away to a safe location and never gave him up. He lived another six months, walked again, and had quality of life before he passed away peacefully in his sleep.

Officer G. testified in the trial that the dog looked fine to him even while admitting to carrying him into the vet's office for me. (OK, call me crazy, but if the dog was fine, why would you need to carry him into the vet's office?)

Poor Doogie, left to die chained in the middle of the yard.
I thought he was dead already when I first saw him.

I think he was quite happy to let me fry for the Doogie incident, thinking that would put me in my place and get me out of his hair. He was wrong.

Unfortunately, at this point O.G. is the only source of pitiful law enforcement I have available to me, so I have no choice but to make use of his dubious services.

I'm smart enough to realize I can't let my grudge stop me from calling him when there are dogs who are suffering and who are left out in the elements. I'm doubtful he'll do anything, but I have to try.

I leave the message, and attempt to get back to organizational work—the dog still holding first place in my thoughts.

❧

Every day we get calls from people with chained or penned dogs who receive letters and brochures in the mail from us, asking them to make their dogs part of their home and family, and offering our assistance to bring the dog inside.

Today is no exception. It turns out to be a young girl from Nebraska who received a letter, and wants to know why she got it. Here we go...

I launch into my spiel, telling her DDB has a form on the website where people input addresses of chained and penned dogs; from these logs we mail information hoping to educate the caretakers of the dogs to bring them into the home and family.

She tells me her dog lives in the house but her roommate has a dog on a chain and one in a pen. I asked her to give him the information and she says, "He won't care."

I'm told the dogs belong to the roommate's girlfriend, and

the caller wants him to give them up to rescue since the girl-friend left, abandoning them. One is a boxer puppy and the other a pit-boxer mix.

I refer her to Nebraska DDB rep Gayla Hausman who's been doing some impressive work, and tell her that Gayla may be able to find her a nearby boxer rescue, but that the pit-boxer might be harder. Hopefully Gayla will be able to assist her.

∝

Events of today alone leave me with three dogs potentially looking for rescue and no place to put them.

If I could get the malamute, what would I do with her? Will Gayla be able to help the boxer and pit-mix, when we know they need rescue this very minute?

Calls like this come into the organization every day, and there are no immediate solutions because we have so few foster homes. If they want to give up a dog, we pledge to look for a foster home, without knowing when or even if we will find a place to put him/her.

If everyone fostered just one dog, just ONE; how much easier would rescuers lives be, how many more dogs would be helped, happy, and rehomed?

How much better would you feel about yourself if you could be part of such an important solution to a nation-wide problem?

Chapter 2

NO EXCUSES: EVERYONE CAN FOSTER, IF EVEN JUST ONE DOG PER LIFETIME

℘

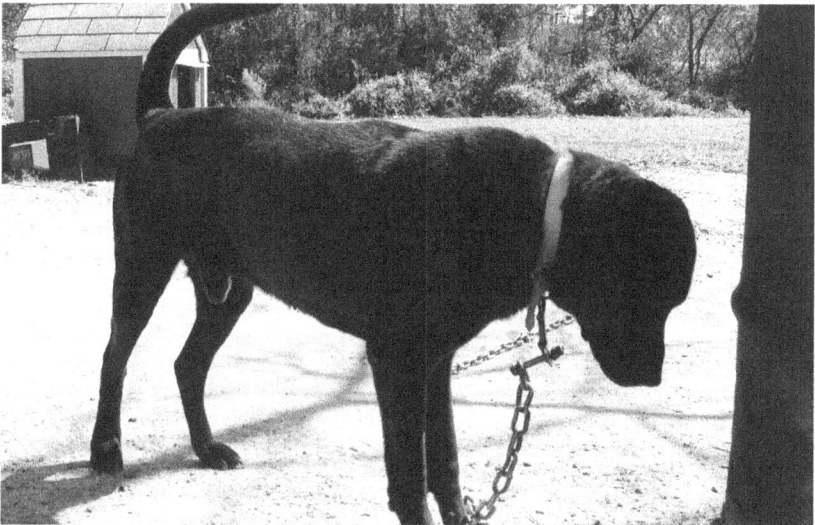

It took two years to free Chippy, but we finally did it!

Truth: We all have reasons WHY we can't foster. I call them excuses.

Tip: Whatever your reason for not fostering, it's nothing you can't get past with a little effort, if only once in your lifetime. Who can't commit to one little dog? Just do it. For them.

Repeat after me: I can always get another husband or wife. Fostering a dog is uber-important and makes a huge differ-ence in our world. It will make me feel like a million bucks and makes a sad dog happy. I'm doing it!

∞

Luckily, when I started DDB I had recently released hus-band #3 (I never said I was good at relationships), I owned my home (well, me and the bank—mostly the bank), and had only my two kids, two dogs, and some cats here and there to worry about.

There was no valid reason I couldn't foster—except it was hard work, inconvenient, and I didn't want to do it. **Wasn't there someone else whose job this was?**

When I succeeded in freeing Worthless and his yardmate Chance from their chains and brought them to my house, I immediately mounted a nationwide search and put out an all points bulletin for someone to take them in. Anyone but me!

I called the few rescue contacts I had, but they were all full. How rude! What was wrong with these people? Did they truly expect me to foster my own rescues? Why weren't they galloping in on their white horses to take this mess I'd made off my hands?

I considered taking them to the Humane Society, but I knew they were high kill, and I couldn't live with that. I wasn't quite that deep in It's-All-About-Me-Land.

I understood real quick-like that there's no point to 'rescu-ing' a dog if you're just gonna dump him or her in the shelter.

Shelters by their very nature engender high stress reactions in dogs, and many rescue groups pull dogs out of shelters every day to save their lives.

Me with Bo (formerly Worthless.) My very first chained-dog rescue and the reason I started Dogs Deserve Better.

Worthless and Chance were both unneutered males, and being so new to the rescue world, I didn't realize what a bad thing that was. For me. Chained dogs are rarely house trained, and the males feel it's their duty to pee on everything in sight as a way to mark their territory...couches, chairs, your leg. No matter.

After hours of crazed-lunatic chasing of dogs around my house, gnashing of teeth, pulling of hair, and spritzing of everything, I recognized the truth: I HAD taken responsibility for these dogs when I took them off the chain, and no one would be coming to save me.

Dammit!

I was forced to shift from "I can't do this, [insert excuse here]" to "I guess I'm doing this, but HOW do I do it without losing it?" What was going on was not working.

I belonged to a yahoo discussion group at the time (remember those?) and I pled for advice on how to contain two leg-lifting, unruly male dogs who were yellow-coating (furniture and walls), fighting (my dogs and each other), and destroying (just about everything) so that I could forego strangling both myself and them.

Admittedly, it would have been hard to strangle myself, but I was about ready to give anything a go by that point.

The group members held my hand as much as possible over the internet, advised me to buy two crates—immediately—and in the end saved my sanity and helped me save the dog's lives. I am grateful to them, to say the least.

If I could buckle down, stop whining, and get the job done, so can you.

I know, I hear it already, the excuses...

I already have a dog. [So does everyone else. In fact, most foster homes claim well more than one dog as 'theirs'.]

My dogs don't like other dogs. [Neither do anyone else's.]

My house is too small. [But not for you and your dog?]

I have to work. [Don't we all.]

And the first-place winner is—drumroll please—I can't foster because my husband or wife won't allow it. [Won't allow it? Don't even get me started.]

I hear it over and over again. In fact, if I had a nickel for every time I've heard these five excuses, I'd be laying on a beach in Hawaii by now. Seriously.

Now that I'm married to husband #4 (this one seems to be sticking, knock on wood—seven years together and I still like him), I've realized that it's actually positive in a relationship for one person to have boundaries where the other doesn't. But you're talking some serious boundary overkill if you can't foster just one little dog until it gets a home.

One a year? Or even one a lifetime?

Relationships are built by two people, and if one has absolute dominion over the other, it's time to rethink the relationship. I know, just ask me, the relationship expert.

I'll be honest with you, my hubby is the Boundary King. He's not overly keen on me fostering dogs now that we actually live in the same house (he was much less vocal about it when it was MY house and we were just dating. Funny how that happens.)

But, he knows me. He knows the woman he married, and he knows that he can't stand in the way of something that I feel strongly about.

If I want to foster a dog, I'll foster a dog.

But I no longer foster five dogs.

That's the compromise, and it works for me.

If you need me to write you a note giving you the thumbs up as the self-titled Queen-of-Foster-Permission-Giving, drop me a line, and I'll zip one over to you.

In fact, I'll make you a deal. If you, as a result of reading this book, foster just ONE dog in your ENTIRE lifetime, I will give you this Get Out of Fostering Free Card. That means, you foster ONE dog, keeping him/her in your home until adoption, and when you again feel pressured to foster, you can flash this card, saying with a bittersweet note of regret in your voice, "Alas, I've already done my time. Here's my card. So sorry, old chap. Pip pip cheer-i-o."

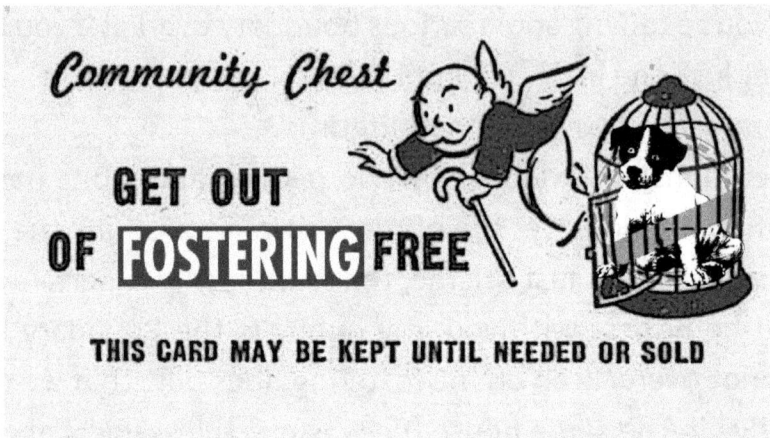

You are then free to meander about and surf the internet instead. Work for you?

The catch is you gotta suck it up and DO it once...no giving back the dog to the rescue group because he licked the peanut butter off your morning toast. No dumping her in the night-drop box at the pound because you won't spend one more minute with the baying hound from Hell...You take her on, get her house-trained, people-trained, doggie-trained, even monkey-trained if need be, and then placed with a new, loving—inside—home and family.

And then? **You Get Out of Fostering FREE.** Woohoo.

P.S. The hubby keeps trying to give me the cards. I told him they don't work for him. Just you. See how special you are?

14

Foster Diary: I was hoping against hope that the malamute's caretakers would call last night and want some help for her, but no such luck.

Silence.

The humane officer leaves a message on the machine that he had been to this residence already in the spring, and the dog was under a doctor's care for the tumor. A doctor's care, my bungus! I wish I could say I'm surprised, but I'm not.

I feel so bad for this innocent dog who is sentenced to remain outside through another cold Pennsylvania winter. Will she survive it? How much will she suffer?

And now I have to be the bad guy who tells the poor neighbor—who actually stepped outside his comfort zone to try to get help for her—that I've failed. They're both screwed.

Our society's treatment of "Man's Best Friend" really sucks.

Chapter 3

YOU'RE NOT CRAZY: FOSTERING IS TOUGH!

⅋

Banshee in the snow, waiting for me to throw the ball. Always.

Truth: Fostering may well be one of the hardest things you'll ever do.

Tip: There are those out there who act like fostering is a piece of cake; ignore them. Either they are that one in a million human who has the patience of a god, or their denial is so deep it looks and smells like doo-doo.

Repeat after me: Fostering isn't easy. It's ok to feel like I'm not good at it. It's ok to feel like I'll never be good at it. I'm doing it anyway.

℘

You probably don't have the patience of a god. If you do, go to the head of the class.

If not, you're just like me in that respect, so take it a little easy on yourself. You still can foster, you still need to foster; you just don't have to do it right all the time or perfectly all the time.

Just doing it will suffice.

Any questions?

Foster Diary: Banshee is another black Lab, this time a purebred (if those sorts of things mean anything to you) who came off a chain 1/2 hour from my home, in Fallentimber, Pennsylvania. I'd been watching him for over a year, since my mom moved his way, as he lay lethargically on the blacktop near his wooden doghouse. He never bothered to raise his head when I passed by, like he'd given up on life.

I literally pass 10 or more chained dogs on the 24-mile trip to Mom's new house; last year my gift to these dogs on Christmas morning was to set up a yard sign near every one of these homes. Until Banshee was given up, my actions only netted me a coupla' nasty phone calls, but now I've rescued 1 out of 10 of these dogs!

To you, that might not be anything to cheer about, but since that's better than my normal rate of success, I choose to be happy about it.

Happy about it, that is, until I'm actually stuck with Banshee. He was initially accepted into a Lab rescue (because he had papers), but instead of a foster home he went to a kennel where he didn't do well, exhibiting signs of aggression.

They dumped him back on us. With nowhere else for him to go, I ended up fostering him here with me.

Banshee and I have a love/hate relationship.

He loves me, and I hate him.

OK, that's not entirely true. I love him when he's being true to himself, giving himself over to what he's meant to do. You'd love him then, too.

Banshee absolutely adores swimming and fetching balls out of the water, and will do it all day long, every day if you let him. He thinks it's his job, and watching him brings nothing but joy. My heart melts watching him fetch that ball, never losing an ounce of enthusiasm for his 'job,' and I mentally compare the image of him sitting on his chain in the dirt, not a single toy in sight, with this new one of him running and playing nonstop in the river near my home.

These moments of bliss make dealing with him worthwhile.

That's the easy part, the love part. The hate part comes in the other 23 hours of the day.

Banshee can only be described as forceful; he's the most pigheaded dog I've ever met, and I've met a lot of dogs. He wants to go with me, everywhere, so badly that he will shove me out of the way to get out the door first, just to make sure I'm not thinking of leaving him behind.

To say I don't like to be pushed around, especially by a male—whether they be human or animal—would be an understatement. It's one of my hot buttons, for sure.

Banshee's pushiness seems to be very dominant behavior, but then suddenly, at the drop of a hat, he'll roll over in submission. He confounds me. He's perfectly fine with the other foster dogs, rarely fights or growls unless they start it, but if he sees a person or another dog when we're out he will sometimes growl and act like he's going to attack. He's unpredictable.

I sent him with Heather, a DDB employee, to a dog training seminar in Ohio, but he came back exactly the same dog. She said he was excellently behaved while he was there—apparently the challenge, the constant interaction, and one on one attention is what the boy needs and craves. This, however, is a problem for me given that I'm routinely fostering at least 5-6 dogs, and have a national organization to run too.

I don't fancy myself a dog trainer, despite all the dogs I've fostered. I've muddled through the best I can, but it doesn't come easy to me. I content myself with the fact that every rescue dog who is lucky enough to end up in my home is getting more, much more, than he/she had out on the end of that chain; for now that has to be enough.

Most fosters quickly find their way to sleeping in my bedroom, and I have built two fenced areas and two doggie doors to accommodate the fosters. They can come inside and out as needed or wanted, and they have lots of dog beds, lots of toys, and lots of love between me, DDB's two employees, my kids, and the occasional volunteer who comes to hang out with them.

Banshee and I will have to keep on muddling through to the best of our abilities. For today, that means we're settling for imperfect.

Chapter 4

CRAPPY HOMES HAPPEN: EVEN WITH THE BEST OF INTENTIONS

&

Maxine was dumped by her humans and attacked by a bear in the West Virginia mountains, living to tell the tale. She got a wonderful home with a Virginia dentist and his family.

Truth: No matter how hard you try to find the very best home for your foster dog, sometimes crappy homes happen.

Tip: Too often for your own comfort you will place dogs in homes that you think will love that dog forever. They won't. No matter how skilled you are at placing dogs, it still happens to the best of us. Forgive yourself. Try again.

Repeat after me: I'm not in control of every result, and I'm doing my very best for my fosters. I love them, then I let them go to what I pray is the perfect home for them. I work through any consequences to the best of my ability.

❧

Crappy homes have happened to me more times than I'd care to admit, and the guilt and the self-blame can be overwhelming. It sucks. While it has gotten better with time and an enhanced ability to see through posers, it still happens to me, and I'm well aware that it can happen with any adoption even when I feel certain my instincts are right.

Unless you're psychic, it already has or will happened to you too when you choose an adopter for your foster dog. Good people tend to blame themselves when other people screw up, but we have to remember that it's not our fault when an adopter returns a dog a day, week, or even a year down the road.

As long as you've been honest and disclosed fully every challenge to a successful adoption, the fault lies solely with the new family who has, for whatever reason, given up on the dog.

If we dwell in the negativity of self-blame or blame of the adopters, we only make ourselves and the dogs miserable.

Just fix the situation the best you can; take the dog back, get him/her into a new foster home, or whatever you need to do to put the safety of the dog first.

But don't let it take away your confidence in yourself!

Should it stop us from fostering? No! Should it take away our belief that we can find new, loving, inside homes for our fosters? No!

You're doing your best, understand that; realize it happens to everyone, and keep on movin'.

Foster Diary: It's Saturday as I write this, a day that many in America have off. Off? What's that? As most of us know, there's not much off-time in the rescue world! The truth is that foster dogs need care every day; it's not just a Monday-Friday, 9-5 commitment.

I'm excited today, though, because I'm taking some time out for one of my favorite pastimes—the movies! I usually justify this two hours of escape at least once a week or so. My daughter Brynnan and I are planning to catch a 1:00 p.m. showing of a movie we actually agree on—that is, right after I meet Sweet Pea's new adopter in State College.

Sweet Pea, of course, is a dog, and a second go-round foster at that, having come back from her so-called 'perfect' home two weeks ago. Another adoption failure.

She was one of what I termed 'the Georgia 30' dogs that area rep Pam Cheatham took on, and quite the job it was. Thirty dogs, mostly inter-related, ended up on chains in a very poor community in Georgia with a couple who, although well-intentioned, was in way over their heads and had no idea what these dogs needed.

As people dropped off animals and the owners attempted to care for them, they just built another pen (even for cats) or chained them up to another doghouse. In the end it turned out to be a huge mess, and they finally agreed to accept help when it became overwhelming.

Pam and some other volunteers built fencing for the couple, who actually got in there and worked right alongside; they gave a whole heap of dogs up to rescue, and agreed to getting the rest spayed or neutered as soon as possible.

I fostered three of these dogs myself and got two more into another DDB foster home in Maryland; others went to various and sundry area reps and other rescue groups.

The three dogs I fostered from this situation were all obviously related, they looked so much alike, all like mini yellow labs with pointy ears. Tiny, 30-lb. dogs, they resembled the dogs you see in third world countries—dogs that don't seem to have a breed, but someone-oughta'-make-up-a-name-for-them-'cause-they're-everywhere.

These dogs have fantastic temperaments.

I fostered Sweet Pea about a year and a half ago, and she was adopted by what we thought was a decent family. Sweet Pea is SO DAMN EASY that if you can't handle her, you can't handle any dog; she's a very-few-issues dog. She is incredibly sweet, a bit on the shy side but nothing you can't work through.

This family lives in downtown Altoona, where I don't generally like to adopt because we get so many returned—but the home visit ascertained the place to be clean, well-decorated, with other nice-looking pets. I believe there was a cat or two, two ferrets, and a couple birds.

In the space of one month this family adopted Bandit, a formerly-chained yellow Lab mix fostered by longtime volunteer Robyn Fanelli, Sweet Pea, and a calico cat, both fostered by me. The woman in the home was very into helping Dogs Deserve Better and wondering what more she could do to make a difference.

Her good intentions quickly faded.

One by one, each of these pets came back. Bandit was first, for getting into the garbage, which we had warned her about before adopting him out. Then the cat came back (just like the song); and finally, a year and a half later, poor little Sweet Pea came back, for peeing in the bedroom.

By this time I'd SO had it with these people. Sweet Pea was absolutely traumatized, from what I don't know. There was no joy left in her, whereas she used to have happiness oozing from her every pore! She was so full of excitement she'd prance like a dancing horse when she saw me coming, bending her little wrists as she lifted each paw high in the air. She brought a smile to my heart.

When they brought her back she cowered and ran the other direction to hide.

Don't underestimate the frustration I felt, I always feel, when this happens. I'd like nothing more than to pummel these people, but obviously I can't do that for all the usual reasons which sane people know and which escape me at the moment.

I knew all I could really do is try harder to make sure she gets the home she deserves next go-round.

[Repeat after me...gotta let it go...gotta let it go....]

I'm hopeful I've done better this time, for Sweet Pea. Her potential new home is past Harrisburg, about three hours drive from my house, so my friend and DDB supporter Gordon Bakalar volunteered to do the home visit for me. He was very impressed with the family and the environment.

He had pledged to be tough, too, because he hung with me and Sweet Pea the weekend before at Woofstock, fell in love with her himself, and had called the Mrs. to tell her he was bringing Sweet Pea home to live with them.

That didn't fly, however, and he went home dogless, echoes of my laughter and ribbing about who wears the pants in the family still ringing in his ears.

Sweet Pea's new mom, Cherie Smith, works from home, and so will be there most days with Sweet Pea and her doggie sister. Cherie's husband Craig and son Justin are eagerly awaiting the newest member of the family, too—just as it should be.

It's shaping up to be a fresh start for Miss Sweet Pea—only two weeks back in rescue and already into a new home! It could be a personal best.

Brynnan and I are to transport her 45 minutes to State College, where we will meet Sweet Pea's new dad and brother. I arrive 10 minutes late because I couldn't get Brynnan out the door on time (she's one of those the-more-you-nag-the-slower-she-moves kids), but they are calm and enthusiastic to see their new family addition and not bothered by our late arrival.

I feel a bit emotional about letting Sweet Pea go again. She really is sweet, and I have a hard time getting over the guilt about her last home despite knowing logically that I did my best. I want to assure her she will always be safe and loved from this day forward. No more pain. Short of keeping her and every other foster I bring in there's nothing I can do but release her and trust. Again.

I give her a really big hug, and with breaking voice, tell her I love her and I pray I did right by her this time.

Craig assures me that this home will be her last, and I am soothed by his gentle tone and kind demeanor into believing it really will be ok.

Two days later I get the following e-mail from Cherie: "We wanted to thank you so much for the opportunity to adopt Sweet Pea. She is truly a sweetheart and when she smiles, it just lights up our lives. Even though she has been with us for only two days, she has fit in and lets us know that she wants lots of love and attention. I spent most of the night cuddling with her on our bed and petting her. She just wanted to be held, and when I stopped petting her, she would nudge me with her nose. You are doing a great thing by rescuing dogs and rehabilitating them so they can be part of a family."

Sweet Pea wanted love from her new family; what a change from when she first came back to me! I could barely touch her, she ran in fear...and then after only two weeks back in a safe environment, she already trusted new people enough to ask for the attention she wanted. I am continually amazed by the way dogs bounce back.

With Sweet Pea gone, I'm back to six dogs in the house. One less dog is something to look forward to, but I wonder how I snuck back up to seven again anyway?

Chapter 5

DOGS ARE LIKE KIDS: THEY REQUIRE SUPERVISION

⅋

Rescued chained dog Tanner did great in a hotel room, but I was smart enough not to leave him alone in the room without a crate. That was a lesson I'd already learned the hard way.

Truth: Dogs are really no different than kids; they require supervision and you will pay the price if you leave them on their own before you know them well enough and they understand what you expect from them.

Tip: Analyze your new foster quickly to figure out how much supervision the new guy will need; some need a lot more than others, especially if they are not housetrained.

Repeat after me: My new foster is my responsibility, and I understand that all dogs are not the same and require different levels of care. I will evaluate the dog and do my best to keep him/her safe.

❧

I've learned the supervision lesson the hard way, and then went back and repeated it again ad nauseam; apparently it's a hard lesson. For me at least. I think it's sunk in, but then the next foster does something so surprising and strange it knocks me for a loop, and I'm back to square one, trying to figure out how I didn't read the needs of the foster correctly.

Banshee is a huge example of my failure to succeed at Tip #5 (you'll discover more in subsequent chapters), but there've been many others. I'm inordinately fond of akitas, who are inordinately fond of attacking other animals, usually without the slightest indication of what is about to go down. At least to my unsophisticated doggie radar.

This failure to contain them has resulted in injury and heartache, making it important to remind myself repeatedly that these dogs need more supervision than I tend to give them. Unfortunately, it's not true of dogs that if they get along one day they will always get along—just like people—and it makes it very difficult to ascertain how much supervision and separation of dogs is needed.

When I traveled the country working conferences, speaking, and running Dogs Deserve Better booths, the dogs were left alone more of the day than I was comfortable with.

The employees would take turns coming in as necessary, staying during work hours, and splitting weekends and evenings for visits throughout the day, but as we had a revolving door of foster dogs, the pack wasn't as stable as it should have been and there were often challenges that arose.

We endeavored to discover immediately how each new foster dog interacted with other dogs, how to keep them separated if need be, and how to meet their needs when I was gone.

In fact, if at all possible before committing to foster a dog, we'd ascertain if he/she was good with dogs and cats, and if not we would try to find another foster home—they required more supervision than we were able to give them.

It's important that you set up a similar system, establish the boundaries of what you can take in, and revise your plans accordingly.

Foster Diary: Speaking of supervision, today I'm lucky enough to be meeting with my parole officer. Part of my so-called punishment for rescuing Doogie—the old shepherd mix left to die on the end of a chain that I mentioned before—is that I get to visit this guy monthly, and even have to get permission slips in order to leave the state. Like a child.

Yet those who left Doogie there to die on a chain in their yard? They got nothing, of course.

To continue the story I started earlier, I was convicted of misdemeanor theft for stealing 'a piece of property'—in this case Doogie—who was left to die at the end of a chain. It was a big hullabaloo, with months of court appearances and a three day trial where the judge and DA accused me of doing it all for publicity....because yeah, that sounds like fun.

Having my name dragged through the mud by the district attorney, lying police officers, and a judge who prohibited the jury from viewing the video of Doogie (which clearly showed him suffering and unable to stand) is something I couldn't conceivably engineer. I'm not that talented.

It was a year and a half of Hell.

Since then I've had lots of time to reflect on this conviction and farce of a trial, and I'm more convinced than ever that I took the only morally justifiable action. The only action that allowed me to sleep at night.

My parole officer is a bit of an odd duck, I can't really figure him out. He loves dogs, has a chocolate Lab, and he spends most of our session talking about dogs. I'll get the feeling that he agrees with me, but then he suddenly turns on me and treats me like a common thief. I think he's so ingrained in the system that he sees everyone as criminals as long as the powers that be see them as criminals. He puts aside what he knows in his heart to take on that mentality, and his actions stem from this black and white thinking.

Today he's complaining because I've only done 28 hours community service (cleaning library shelves because the judge said that "people are dogs too"), and I'm supposed to have 300 hours done in the next four months.

With proper vet care and medication in foster care, Doogie was able to walk and even run again. He was worth the suffering.

I ask him, "Why is it fair that someone who kills a dog gets

16 hours community service (true story), but someone who saves a dog gets 300?" He says, "It was the method you used. Taking the dog without the owners' permission."

Oh, that. I ask him what method he might suggest to get immediate help for a dying dog when the owner and the humane officer failed in their duties to provide him the care he needed and deserved?

No answer.

Honestly, I wonder how these people sleep at night.

I'm on my way home, and I pass the dog I'm most-currently stressed about, whose name, I eventually learn, is Kanook. He's one I've been itching to rescue—a long-haired shepherd that I first noticed on the chain, and have watched for about two years. He and his yardmates, a chow chow and a min pin, used to live chained to doghouses, but after we gave them a brochure and a poster-war ensued (I hang posters and put signs near their house—they go out and rip them down—repeat ad infinitum), she decided that putting a pen on her porch would be the better alternative. No outside shelter at all now.

Wow, that's better! Not.

Looking on the bright side, I think the dogs do spend some time in the house now, so that would indeed be progress. I notice that sometimes the pen seems to be empty.

But, this shepherd and several min pins still spend most of their time out on the porch in this pen, together, milling about in an 8x8 area.

I've been noticing the shepherd getting skinnier and skinnier, at least I think so but I don't have a good view from the road. There's normally no one home at this time of the day, so I determine that I'm going to get a better look to see if he's really that bad.

I pull off and start snapping pictures from the road, and I see the blinds lift as someone looks out at me. "Crap," I say to myself. I'm not trespassing, so there isn't much she can do about it. Theoretically. I brace myself for the coming confrontation.

She opens the door and demands "What're you doing?"

Luckily—or unluckily—by this time I've realized the dog is a skeleton, and I'm so horrified that she is immediately nice to me to stave off trouble for starving the dog. I hold my hand to my mouth and say, "Oh God, I'm taking pictures of that dog, he's a skeleton, what is going on here?"

She comes outside and I meet her on the porch where the dogs are in the pen. She says "Is he really that skinny? He eats like a pig, but he doesn't gain any weight. I think he's just growing."

I'm sick! The min pins look in ok shape, but the shepherd is horrendous. I just want to feed him, feed him, feed him before it's too late.

I tell her there's no way that's normal; he needs help right away. I think he's going to die if he doesn't get help, and soon.

Maybe he has Exocrine Pancreatic Insufficiency (if she is feeding him as she claims), which means he doesn't have any enzymes to digest his food. If that's the case, even though he eats and eats, his food will come out the other end without him getting any nutrients from it; he will eventually starve to death.

I see a couple yellow cow-patties in the pen, something I later learn is typical of the disease.

She appears to be genuinely upset by this point, and doesn't want her dog to die. (Fair warning, one of the biggest lessons I've learned in this work—people who abuse animals lie through their teeth, and are very good at making you believe whatever bullshit they tell you. Trust me, it's the truth. Go try rescuing for awhile. They lie, and you believe them because you can't imagine they could look you in the eye and lie so blithely, but they can and they do, and you will believe them again and again until you've been made a fool of so many times you start to take every story with 100 grains of salt. Really.)

She says she wants to help him, but she's going through a divorce and she doesn't have the money to treat him. We handwrite a lame-o agreement—she won't sign a release form—that if he doesn't have the disease we will work with her to get him healthy, and she will keep him inside more.

Of course I'm hoping she just lets the poor dog go, lets us keep him, but it's doubtful. People who abuse animals are quite persistent when it comes to keeping their property to continue to abuse as they see fit. It's a power trip thing.

We make an emergency vet appointment for Kanook at 3:15 p.m., at the same vet where I have to pick up Magnum, another formerly-chained foster, from a punch biopsy to investigate a diagnosis of Pemphigus, an autoimmune disease that erupts in blisters in the mouth and between the feet.

I take Kanook to the vet, and despite his skeletal structure, scabs, and fleas, they don't find anything wrong with his bloodwork. I asked for him to be tested for EPI, though, and now I think they ignored me and just did regular blood testing.

That's annoying! I feel convinced he has this disorder, and now I have to figure out how to get nourishment into his system, and fast.

The dog is just bones, but he's starting to try to play with me, which is touching but sad—he's so unsteady on his feet even while he's playing because he doesn't have any nutrition to keep him going!

Hello, people...really big dog, weighs 63 pounds, should weigh at least 95 pounds...who doesn't get the message that there's something wrong with this picture?

Chapter 6

FOSTER DOGS DESTROY THINGS: HEED THE WARNING

℘

George played nicely with his gift during a Girl Scout visit.
As soon as they left, he promptly shredded it to pieces. Next!

Truth: When you foster a dog, especially a former 'outside' dog, (although there is no such breed), things in your home WILL get destroyed.

Tip: Figure out as quickly as possible what must be done to safely contain a destroyer before everything in your home is demolished. For every dog there is a different solution. Don't just sit around and whine about it, take action.

Repeat after me: For my sanity and the preservation of things I value, I will become proactive. Contain and prevent, contain and prevent, seal off from sensitive areas!

∞

I've had more damage done to my home and possessions through fostering than I could ever myself manage in my wildest, teenagiest, drunkennest days. I went through so many sofas, even having three different ones donated by a local store, that I ended up giving up on sofas altogether until I moved to Virginia with my hubby three years ago. My living room became all dog beds and office equipment, and my stress level went down because there was less destruction.

Of course, there was no place to sit then but the floor.

I remember buying one small couch, it was more of a large two-person chair really, at a yard sale for $40.00 one summer. I covered it constantly with old donated hotel bedspreads to try to protect it from the wreckage, and I wondered if it would make it 'til the next summer when I could find another at a yard sale again. It didn't.

I can't wait to go through photos from the early days of Dogs Deserve Better, so I can remember what my house looked like when I started fostering. I remember seeing a photo of an Italian professor I briefly dated at the beginning of Dogs Deserve Better, and he was sitting in a room that looked lovely—it was decked out with plants, clean floors, and a shiny, well turned-out table. I wondered where the photo was taken...then I realized it was my former dining room.

Yikes! I had no idea how far my house had gone downhill.

Dawn Ashby, fellow rescuer and former DDB employee, is full of stories about the destruction of her home and family furnishings by foster dogs. I imagine these stories are funny only in hindsight, but she has a gift with story-telling, so I'm always rolling when she regales me with them.

Her husband, we'll call him Darin 'cause that's his name, used to be very anti-fostering himself, which to Dawn's credit she studiously ignored as much as possible. He can be a teensy bit blustery, it seems, when faced with damage done by a foster dog, and Dawn had a foster who regularly ate a hole in the wall. A different spot each day.

So she and her daughters would rearrange the furniture every day before he got home from work to cover up the latest hole until the next day when they could get out to get some patching supplies.

He'd wonder aloud each night why they were suddenly so obsessed with rearranging the room, and she'd tell him they just couldn't find the way they liked it best!

When we met up in Chicago for a DDB Chain Off Event, Dawn left her foster dog Heidi in my hotel room for a few hours—nevermind why she didn't have her own hotel room—while we filled goody bags for the event the next morning.

Heidi, left to her own devices and apparently not in agreement with this plan, took it upon herself to attempt an escape, digging up the carpet in front of the door, eating the door frame, and peeing in the middle of the floor for good measure and to show Dawn just how truly annoyed she was to be left alone.

I was quite flustered about it; but Dawn's family acted like it was just another day at the office. They trooped off en masse to the local hardware store, bought some putty, wall paint, and fabric paint, and fixed the room before making their way back home to see what may have gone awry back at the ranch while they were absent.

I can't poke too much fun at Dawn's dogs, though, because I fostered a blind akita named Bridget who did the exact same thing to me in a hotel room in Harrisburg, Pennsylvania at the first ever Puppymill Awareness Day. I was absolutely horrified upon coming back to the room to discover the damage, and was out in the middle of a torrential downpour buying two different kinds of glue to put the wallpaper back together, jigsaw style.

When you foster, these sorts of catastrophes and disasters may and probably will befall you too; get your head in the game, fix what you can, and throw out the rest. And pay the hotel when you get caught.

Make a new plan to safely contain your unruly boy or girl so that your stress level can reduce back to pre-mayhem stage. Remember we've all been there, you're not alone!

And—maybe the best tip you'll get in this whole book— take it from Dawn and me: always, always, ALWAYS use a crate when staying in a hotel room with your foster dog if you have to step out for even a second! This is a crucial sanity tip, do not ignore it—you will pay the price in both mental stability and hotel fees if you don't. It's not worth it.

Foster Diary: Banshee's now out of tennis balls, having easily gone through four a day, and he let's me know he's bored this morning by starting to grab and chew other items that he finds and shouldn't be chewing, such as plastic bottles, cans, and shoes.

Banshee can destroy a tennis ball in under 30 seconds. Luckily, he doesn't seem inclined to actually swallow them. He's obsessed with them, though, and if you have one, he wants it, no exceptions. I wish he weren't so hard on them, and so slobbery and disgusting about it. I would be happy to throw them for him while I work, but they are either sopping wet or so demolished they can't even be thrown. Yuk.

Happily, Banshee and the other dogs are all doing fine with Kanook, which kinda' surprises me. With Banshee being so pushy and occasionally dominant, I'm always astonished to see that he's not really bothered by any new foster I drag in.

A trainer told me he just never learned how to interact with other dogs, so he ignores them. Makes sense to me.

I'm spending way too much time googling for symptoms and solutions for Skelly, my new nickname for Kanook, which is short for Skeleton of course. My research last night indicated that if he does have EPI, he shouldn't have any food with grains, which cuts out most dog foods.

I'm trying to buy some enzymes over the internet, but turns out you need a prescription, which I totally don't get… it's just enzymes!

In case you don't know, enzymes are what help the body to break down food. Since we normally produce our own they aren't necessary, but in Kanook's case he may need them in order for his body to digest the food and provide him with nourishment.

I've fed him twice already adding over-the-counter enzymes which are similar and I'm hoping will at least help him digest something, anything. I fed him my akita's sweet potato and salmon food mixed with enzymes too, no grains.

He's still pooping a lot, though, the sickly-pale yellow poop piles that are characteristic of the disease.

Meg, the vet tech, thinks he has tapeworm with all those fleas, so I tell her I'll be up for some worm meds. I print out info on Exocrine Pancreatic Insufficiency to give doc...I'd like him to give me the prescription for the enzymes based on my research so I can get them immediately.

The worst that can happen is that his body doesn't really need them; they certainly will not harm him, so there's no risk involved in getting the prescription started. In fact, many natural doctors suggest taking supplemental enzymes regularly even if they aren't absolutely necessary because they help your body to digest faster.

They order me the prescription and I should have it tomorrow or the next day. Thank you!

Chapter 7

CRATES AND OTHER TOOLS OF THE TRADE: USE 'EM AS YOU NEED 'EM!

⅋

Say "AAAAH" Copper. Note the six foot solid wall behind him at the DDB Good Newz Rehab Center. This separated the two packs, and if they can't see each other, there is less stress. Theoretically.

Truth: Dogs can be couch potatoes, or not. It's the 'or not' you have to worry about. Sometimes you need tools to help you survive.

Tip: Crates, fences, gates, and doggie doors (as well as your personal favorites) are your friends. Without them you end up a Screaming Banshee. Invest in your sanity.

Repeat after me: My sanity is worth spending a few bucks on tools for doggie containment. Get outta' the way, I'm ordering mine right now!

℮

When I started fostering, I didn't have a fence. Or crates. Or doggie doors. I was not brought up with knowledge about how to be a good dog parent. None of my pets were allowed in the house when I was a kid, and I hated them being outside.

The only thing I knew for sure after seeing the way our pets lived was that chains were bad. Living in the house was good.

All the rest was a gray area that I had to figure out as I went along; this meant I made a lot of mistakes, and then I learned how to do it better.

Of my many mistakes, the first one was allowing foster dogs to run the neighborhood. Not good, and I apologize to the god of foster doggies for this incredibly daft faux pas. Since I didn't have a fence, or the money to buy one, I tended to just open the door and hope they'd come back when they were done. This method rarely ended well for me—angry neighbors, porcupine quills, skunk juice, ripped-up garbage— yeah, it was that bad. And I was miserable.

I know you perfect foster parents are clucking right now and vowing never to give me another foster dog (thank you!), but this is why I believe that people can do better...because I learned, and if I could learn after the childhood I had, then others can too.

I finally sucked it up my second year of work with DDB and spent my entire income tax refund on a fence. It was the best investment in my sanity I ever made! Bar none.

Eventually we had enough fencing donated that we were able to fence another section off the garage-turned-DDB-office, and then we had two areas to separate dogs when necessary. It was a little slice of responsibility heaven!

I also added doggie doors to both sides of the yard, and those have made my life so much better. Some people are against doggie doors, because they don't like dogs going outside when they aren't home for safety reasons. I get that.

For me, though, the benefits outweighed the risks, giving me the freedom to travel as needed, and the dogs the freedom to go out for fresh air and potty breaks as they desired.

I'm not personally a huge fan of crates, because I'm all about the most freedom possible and I hate confining the dogs, but I strongly feel they have a place in dog training and safety. I see them as a tool you can rely on with a new foster until you are able to ascertain how much freedom the dog can tolerate without getting him/herself into trouble.

As the dog becomes more and more sane and less and less dangerous to himself, others, or the furniture, then I prefer to leave the crate unused, waiting for the next dog who needs its services.

Look at the time a dog spends in there as merely an investment in a future free of unnecessary confinement of any kind. But remember—never, never, never leave the dog in there 24/7! That's just horrendous, cruel, and unacceptable.

There are many hoarders who masquerade as rescuers; these folks take in dog after dog to make others think they're saintly. Trouble is, when they take in too many dogs, things DO go completely haywire (this is a 100% certainty). To make their lives easier, these cruel folks throw them in crates and leave them there until they die or wish they were dead.

I led a two-week protest against just this kind of rescuer in the state of Washington in 2013; Steve Markwell had at least 125 dogs crammed in a pink warehouse and NEVER let them out of their crates. EVER.

In the end we were successful in driving him to pack up the dogs in a big truck and get out of town. (If you must know, I did get a teensy little arrest out of it, for protesting after he got a restraining order against us. But they dropped it in exchange for a 'bribe' of $250. At least that's my recollection.)

Luckily in the end he turned them over to another rescue group, and eventually most of the dogs were moved to safety and found homes with rescuers who could meet their needs. We will never know how many dogs died in Steve Markwell's care, but he was never charged with any kind of cruelty to animals. The fact that animal abusers get away with these misdeeds repeatedly is incredibly frustrating and we must make our voices heard to ensure that law enforcement actually does their job.

Please, don't EVER let yourself be this kind of person. Crates are tools only, for temporary use, and the goal should always be to give the dog as much freedom as safely possible.

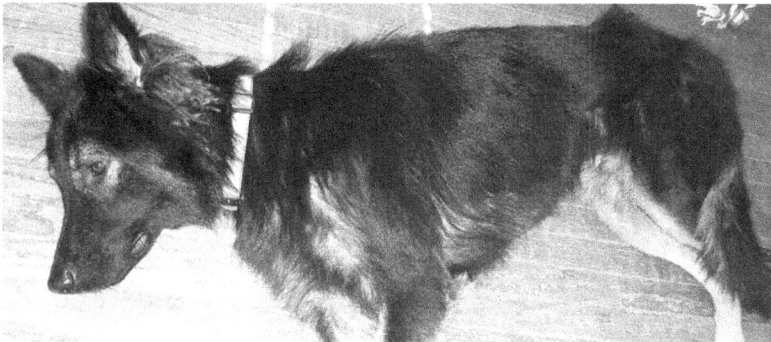

Foster Diary: I've been trying to get Kanook to understand the beauty of the doggie door and the fenced yard, but he apparently doesn't grasp it's full meaning yet.

Case in point, this morning I walked down the steps to an incredible sight: poop! In the middle of my floor! Now, I'm not usually a happy camper when this happens...but today I am excited because it is perfectly formed, dark brown, lovely dog poop! Which means, unless one of the other, completely housetrained dogs decided to take a big dump and blame it on the new guy, Skelly did a normal poop!

Which would mean he's digesting his food!

I'm already falling in love with Kanook—well, I was in love with him from afar for the past two years. But I'm trying not to love him, because I'm afraid that this will end badly. His caretaker doesn't think she did anything wrong, and I don't think she'll release him to me.

I already know how lame the law enforcement is.

❧

Just as I suspected, Kanook's caretaker, Dragon Lady, calls me toward evening and announces she's "coming to get him." We argue for an hour, and I finally convince her to google Exocrine Pancreatic Insufficiency with German shepherd, and call me back to discuss it further after she reads up on it.

I wait uneasily, but she doesn't call back. I'm pissed at myself; I really screwed up in not pushing her harder to give him up. I should have known better than to trust that she would do the right thing.

I was so desperate to get him to the vet that I took any deal I could make, and in the long run I'm afraid it won't be enough for him.

Damn it all.

Chapter 8

DOGS DO LEARN: THE SUPERVISION CAN BE LESSENED OVER TIME

ℬ

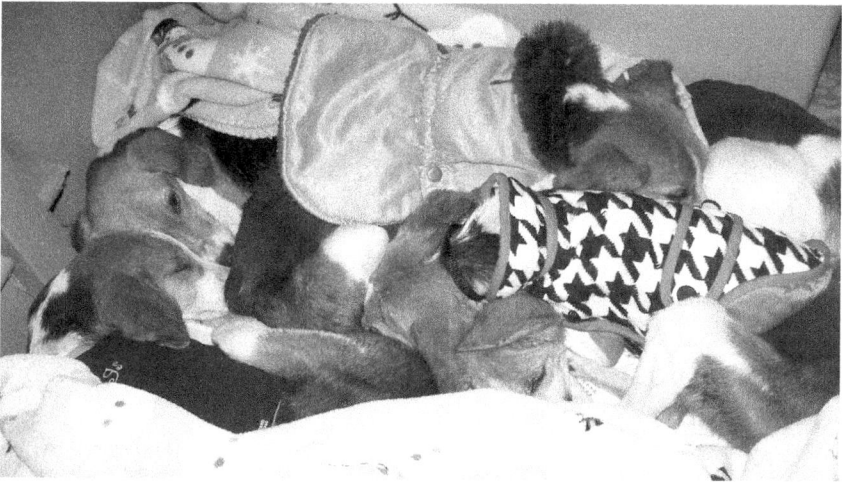

Sure, puppies are cute when they're sleeping…just like kids. But most rescuers will tell you they are among the hardest fosters imaginable—the non-stop pooping, peeing, destruction, and utter mayhem when they're awake make for some tough days while you get them ready for new homes.

Truth: Just like people learn to do better (right?), so can dogs. When you are finished whipping your foster into shape, she will be a prize worthy of any new home. Usually.

Tip: Your foster will become better-behaved with time…if it's hard right now, keep your focus, stick it out; soon enough you will see the fruits of your labor. Remember who's smarter: YOU. You can find a solution to any challenge.

Repeat after me: My foster [insert name here] may be making me crazy right now, but I am smarter, and I will find a solution that works. Soon I won't believe how far we've come together!

❧

When I was fostering Banshee, I was praying that I was smarter than him, because it seemed like we were going backwards instead of forwards! As each day passed he seemed to get even stronger-willed and more energetic.

It was like his muscles had atrophied from all the time on the chain, but with exercise he gained strength and felt better—which only released more and more waves of raw Canine-Destructo power. We had been walking the dogs two miles three-four times a week that fall, but it didn't seem to touch his energy level.

I'd had other fosters that seemed like hopeless cases in the beginning, but after we struggled along and made progress, they had ended up getting wonderful homes and having a grand life. I needed that same miracle for Banshee!

Just remember, lots of dogs start out as maniacs...but when you're through working your magic and building your patience and tolerance muscles, they will do you proud as they run off to their new forever homes, content in the loving arms of their new family.

Either that, or you're stuck with them for life, like that 40-year-old kid that lives in his parents' basement forever. And no one wants that, do we?

Foster Diary: Banshee was just chasing a cat again, I don't like the way he's acting around them. Hopefully it's just part of that new manic energy and will wear off, but in the meantime, I have to watch him. When he first came he ignored the cats, but the past few days he's started to give them the evil eye and chase them around the house. I'm correcting him, stepping between them, and telling him firmly that they are 'mine'; he's an intelligent dog, he should get it.

Kanook, on the other hand, is really quite a breeze to be with, and is a dog that would easily find a great home given half a chance. I wouldn't call him a couch potato, but like most shepherds he's incredibly intelligent and a very fast learner. He's strong-willed, but not dominant, and he listens if you correct him. You can almost see him trying to figure out what you want from him. He brings me joy.

I've decided to take him with me to Ohio to a speaking engagement to buy him a few days. I call Dragon Lady and luckily get her answering machine. I leave a message that I'm going to Ohio for DDB, and was planning to take him with me due to his special needs. Since I haven't heard from her, I'm going to go ahead with that plan, but let her know I'll call her when I get back Sunday or Monday.

I really love the dog already. He's just a damn nice dog. Quiet, always hungry, starvation is the name of his game, but he's also a gentleman, regardless of his driving hunger.

He never grabs the food from my hand even though he probably longs to.

The road trip to Ohio is much further than I expect, and even though we leave at 9:00 a.m., we don't arrive at our destination until almost 5:00 p.m.

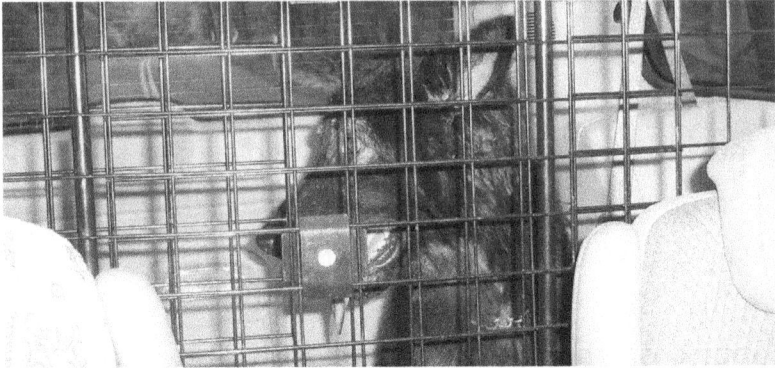

I'm a dilly-dallier when I travel, preferring to drink lots of iced tea and tour the rest areas. Kanook has the whole back of the van to lounge in and plenty of blankets for cushioning his weary bones. I have the safety divider installed between him and the middle row of seats so he doesn't get too wild and I can pay attention to the road. I make sure to get him out at the rest areas, offering him food and water each time, although oddly he's not very interested. Traveling is probably a new and unusual experience for him.

I find myself embarrassed to walk him, and try to stop at places where there aren't a lot of people, because I worry that others will believe that I'm the one who mistreated him to this extent. God, NEVER!

When I'm a couple of towns away from Lois Rose's house—our destination for the night—I suddenly see sirens behind me. Crap! I don't know where this guy came from, and at first

I think maybe he wants to get by me and go after the car in front of me...but no such luck.

He pulls me over, and I am scared that the Dragon Lady reported her dog stolen and I would be thrown in the slammer. I know, Doogie flashbacks. Paranoia issues.

But, it boils down to a slight speeding miscommunication—the signs say 55, and I, completely innocently of course, took that to mean 65. I get away with a warning. Thank-ee Jesus! How often does that happen? Maybe he actually agreed with my van signs about dog chaining and believed in my mission. I'm ever the optimist, eh?

Lois Rose, DDB rep and long-time animal advocate, is putting us up for the night because I'm speaking at a local dog event tomorrow. Over a wonderful dinner and some wine I tell Kanook's story for Lois and our fellow dinner guests, and they are shocked and saddened to see him in this emaciated condition.

They are just as taken with that boy as I am; he wins everyone over easily, Lois's dogs included. He's my constant shadow throughout the evening, believing I'm his family even though he's known me only a couple of days. He sleeps soundly on the floor by my bed that night, and has no accidents. What an angel!

Chapter 9

DOGS ARE UNPREDICTABLE: YOU JUST NEVER KNOW, EVEN WHEN YOU THINK YOU KNOW

⅌

Betty White was an old hound who we thought would be happy to laze about all day. She surprised us all by being incredibly playful once she started feeling better. She shivered outside in the cold, so she ended up with eight coats from donors for her very own fashion show. We sent them along to her new home with her...yep, most times even the senior dogs find someone to love them!

Truth: No matter how long you foster or how much of an expert you consider yourself, dogs can and will still take you by surprise. They aren't machines but beings with minds of their own, and they think differently than humans.

Tip: What can you do? Expect the unexpected...learn to be flexible and roll with the punches.

Repeat after me: The more I think myself the expert, the closer I am to a sure fall. I will remain open to surprises and do my best to bounce back when they come along.

❧

I used to believe that all dogs were sweetness and light, and they want nothing more than for humans to pet them and spend time with them; everything else like bathroom breaks, eating, and sleeping came easily. They were angels with fur, incapable of harming or destroying. Boy, was I naive!

Banshee is a stocky Lab with a wide face, favoring the true water dogs. When I first saw him on the chain he scared me; his body language made me nervous. Ever since I was attacked by a chow chow I rescued from a chain—sending me to the hospital in an ambulance—I am extremely leery of approaching a chained dog, especially if it's a large, unneutered male.

I can now fully grasp the reality that dogs are capable of killing me, and though I work through my fear and keep fostering new chained dogs, I have not been able to eliminate the initial wariness from my consciousness.

When I led DDB, we logged children who were attacked and killed or seriously injured by chained dogs on our Parents Against Dog Chaining site, and because of my attack I now have a better idea how they feel. I was terrified and helpless against this dog who was attacking me, afraid I was going to die—and I'm an adult! I can only imagine how terrifying it is to be a young child and see this large dog coming at you, biting you, and having no hope of defending yourself. It's no wonder so many attacked children die as a result—they don't have a chance against a large dog intent on killing.

The only reason I was able to get away without worse injury or death from the chow chow attack was that I thought quickly, and I understood I was in a life or death situation and so my brain engaged. Cyclone backed me into the corner of the kitchen, near the sink where I had pots and pans waiting to be washed, and then lunged. I grabbed a pot and a cookie sheet, using one to shield my body and the other to defend myself against him. He first went for my throat, but missed and got my chest instead. I was lucky that I was wearing a thick sweatshirt and bra, or my injuries in that area could have been debilitating.

Then he grabbed my arm, and finally latched onto my left ankle, shredding it with his canines. This was where I sustained the worst of my injuries. Once I had the pots in hand and could start fighting back, I was able to confuse him enough that he went out the doggie door and I dragged myself over and shut him outside.

My son was 15 at the time, and was home sick from school that day. He heard my screams and started down the stairs, but I yelled for him to go back up, afraid Cyclone would attack him too. I couldn't bear that! Rayne called the ambulance and rode with me to the hospital, and as much as I wish he didn't have to be part of that trauma, I was grateful he was there to help me get the care I needed.

I ended up with stitches on my left ankle in four different places from the dog's fangs tearing my leg. I can only assume he was trying to drag me down to the floor so he could attack me from the dominant position above me. If that had happened, I truly believe he wouldn't have stopped the attack until I was dead.

I was so traumatized afterward that I had nightmares about the dog, and one night I was coming down the steps in the middle of the night for a drink of water and some ibuprofen. There was a chair left in the middle of the floor where one didn't normally sit, and in my mind it was Cyclone crouching into an attack position to come after me again.

I knew at that point I was really messed up over the attack and maybe needed to see a shrink or something. The dog warden who helped me with Cyclone told me he also was attacked by a chained dog, and spent years in counseling to deal with the trauma it caused him. I got it, and I wasn't alone in my anguish.

Cyclone was the only dog I've ever personally put down for aggression, and I still hated to do it. I wished a magical dog trainer would suddenly appear to carry him off to magical dog training land so I didn't have to make the hard choice. But none did, and I had to make the best decision available to me to protect both the people and the animals that lived and worked in my home. If someone died as a result of my failure to make the tough call, that blood would have been on my hands.

The news was all over my dog attack (they were always

interested in the 'bad' stories, but never the good) and so I had to publicly state what happened and the decisions I'd made as a result. I got nasty e-mails from people who judged me for euthanizing Cyclone—the oh-so-perfect people who would have done so much better—but most active rescuers understood what I'd faced and would have made the same decision.

Losing only 1 out of 250 chained foster dogs for aggression is actually an excellent track record, even though in an ideal world I could reach them all. People were so cruel that they blamed me for the attack, claiming that I had somehow instigated it. So not only did I have the pain of my own experience and wounds, and the sadness of having to put Cyclone down, but I was also made to feel guilty like I was somehow at fault for his actions.

If that were truly the case, why did none of the other 249 dogs I rescued from chains attack me? If my actions were faulty, then we would see a pattern of attacks from other dogs I fostered, but most of my rescues were grateful and loving beings just trying their best to be part of the family.

It puts me in mind of the way society blames a woman for her own rape because she dresses too sexily, or a wife's aggravation of her husband for her black eyes. There are no valid excuses for abuse, and just because it's a dog doing it instead of a human doesn't make it any more acceptable.

Dogs are capable of horrific violence against humans just as humans are capable of horrific violence against dogs, and those like me who survive unprovoked dog attacks should never be made to feel it is somehow their fault.

I believe Cyclone's aggressive behavior was innately genetic and aggravated by the territorialism brought on by life on a chain. While many dogs with a tendency toward aggressive behavior get the socialization and training with humans they need at a young age to help them understand what is right and what is wrong, dogs who live chained get no training or socialization with humans. They become up to 3X more likely to attack due to isolation and confinement to a small area, leading to frustration and acting out.

Even though we rescued Cyclone from his chain without incident, he retained his aggressive behavior, perhaps snapping from so long in a horrendous environment.

Ironically, the most vocal critic of me for euthanizing Cyclone was a chow rescuer from Illinois, one we'd approached numerous times in the six months we worked to get him off the chain. We had requested assistance from her rescue multiple times, but she never once stepped up to help.

I've gotten better since then at reading doggie body language, and Banshee's body language on the chain was frightening to me. He lowered his head slightly, ears up, his tail a little above half-cocked, and just stared at me, motionless.

I didn't go near him until his caretaker came out and he relaxed. Then he was a different dog.

While an attack is one behavior you could encounter as a doggie foster parent (and I hope you never do), there are other predictably unpredictable actions your foster dogs might take that will throw you for a loop, such as but not limited to: jumping another dog, seemingly unprovoked (don't reach in, that only gets you bit); climbing or digging out of the fence;

chewing out of the crate; eating things they have no business eating; destroying something meaningful or expensive; slipping out the door and touring the neighborhood, peeing on your best friend, etc., etc.

The best advice I can give you during these times is to think on your feet, roll with the punches, and know that there IS a solution; you just have to find it and implement it. Opening your mind to understanding there is an answer out there will enable you to think more clearly and find an answer more quickly.

The solution may not always be fun, may not even be easy, but you will somehow get through it and eventually the worst of it will be over.

Foster Diary: Dawn and I are both set to speak at the dog walk in Ohio, and I tell Kanook's story to the dog lovers gathered there. While I'm talking, he lays flat on his side on the concrete behind me, and he is so skinny his body looks pasted to the ground, like he's not even three-dimensional. Like a cartoon character who got run over by a bus. It sickens me. I can't even think about the possibility of giving him back.

On the way home from Ohio, I call Heather, who is feeding and caring for the dogs while I'm gone.

She tells me that someone got up on the counter in the kitchen and chewed up a bottle of ibuprofen, but she didn't know who it was. Everyone seemed ok to her when she was there, so she believes that little was actually ingested.

I tell her I'm sure it was Banshee, because I've caught him lately taking plastic containers out of the bathtub, sink, or wherever, so I should have thought that he might get up on the counter and help himself. That isn't good.

I'm very nervous that she didn't take action, and I'm hours away from home myself. Seems to me, and anyone will tell you I'm usually the last one running to the vet in a panic, that this is one of those times there should have been at least a phone call made to an emergency vet.

I hope she's right and try to put it out of my mind for the rest of the trip.

When I get home at 10:30 p.m., absolutely exhausted from the seemingly endless trip home, I give the dogs a little snack and then immediately crawl in bed for what I'm hoping will be a decent night's sleep. I'm just about to fall asleep when I hear the first sounds of puking.

You guessed it, Banshee. He pukes three times during the night, once on each dog bed, and I think that's good, he's getting it out of his system.

Chapter 10

DOGS ARE NEEDY: THEY WILL SUCK THE LIFE OUT OF YOU

ℬ

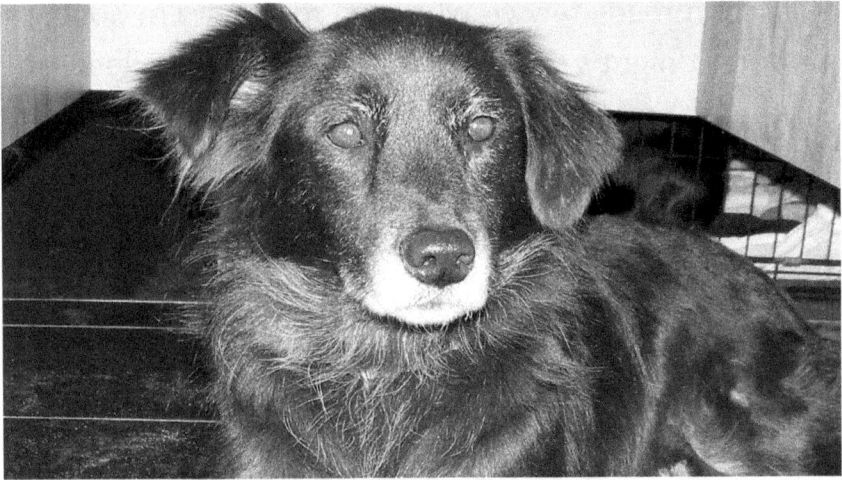

Emma was one of my few exceptions to the neediness rule. She wasn't really shy or feral, but just didn't seem to enjoy human touch. She wanted to be in the same room with you, and lay near you, but if you went to pet her or rub her belly she got stiff as a board. She still found a home where she was accepted for who she was, and that's why honesty is so important when trying to place your dogs...if you lie to a potential new family, you are bound to get the dog returned.

Truth: Dogs are the neediest critters on the planet, bar none. New fosters will be up your butt all day long, every day, and that even includes the bathroom.

Tip: Accept the neediness as part of the package, and know that over time it will lessen. It won't go away totally—it's in the nature of the dog—but the extreme insecurity will diminish.

Repeat after me: The obsession is just temporary; I will firmly shut the door when I pee, and enjoy that one moment of solitude. I'm on my way to creating necessary boundaries.

If you're like me, I'm sure that the neediness of your foster dog or dogs is one of your biggest foster parenting challenges. How do you put boundaries into place so that your sanity remains intact while you're fostering? How do you meet their needs without losing yourself because you have not one moment of solitude?

We need to make ourselves as important as our dogs and our families. For many of us, especially women, we tend to put our children, our pets, and everyone else ahead of ourselves. If your foster dog is too needy, it's time to start creating boundaries. These will actually give the dog more security instead of less, and you more freedom to breathe.

I've fostered many dogs who I'd call velcro dogs, but Banshee by far stands out as the worst. Banshee always had his eyes on me. Every second. I would be working, and he'd just stand beside me, watching me intently. And stand, and stare. It was creepy.

Now maybe if a lover looked at me like that...naw, that would be creepy too.

When Banshee finally got tired of standing and staring, he'd pick up a toy, take it to a doggie bed in the corner, lay his chin on said toy, and keep watch over me constantly from his perch.

Until I moved. Then he'd be up and on me again like white on rice, said toy either forgotten on the bed or dragging along with him in case he could persuade me to throw it.

Banshee was one of the neediest dogs I've ever fostered, but most are similarly needy when they first come into rescue. As foster parents, we logically know this neediness stems from their past unpleasant circumstances. If the dogs lived on a chain, they were incredibly lonely and undersocialized for their entire lives. Knowing this and feeling intense empathy in regards to their former living conditions often leads us to let them to push us around a little too much.

In layman's terms, we feel guilty that they had such crappy lives, so we want to make it all better; as a result we become the doormat. And then we suffer.

I would often troop to the bathroom with four or five dogs

trailing along behind, and that could get damn irritating. If I didn't totally latch the door, Banshee would push it open with his nose and tromp in, looking at me like, "Don't worry, Mom, I know you didn't mean to shut me out, but I got it open, so we're all good now."

Remember it will get better—well, with normal dogs who aren't Banshee—because most fosters over time decide you are capable of going to the bathroom by yourself. They'll only follow you when there's hope that something really exciting is about to happen—like driving the car, fixing a snack, or going outside to scoop poop. Then, your chances of leaving them behind are slim to none.

Remind yourself how nice it is that they love you so much. Really, what people actually want to spend this much quality time with you?

Foster Diary: In the morning Banshee seems more laid back and calmer than normal, but he's still up and walking around and eats his breakfast.

I call the vet who does all our spays and neuters, and tell them what happened. The vet tech, Meg, says that since he threw up he should be fine, but keep our eye on him for any signs of worsening, and fingers crossed he'll bounce back.

He later throws up two more times, but otherwise doesn't act overly sick.

In worse news, I had to let Kanook go today. Part of me doesn't even want to talk about it, or write about it, I'm so ripped up over it. But here it is, the whole wretched story . . .

When I got back from Ohio and listened to the messages,

there was a call from Dragon Lady saying she didn't threaten me (I guess telling me she's going to turn the case over to the police isn't threatening?) and that she was just upset, but she can take care of him herself.

The way she's been doing?

It was late, so I didn't call her back, but went to bed determined to call the humane officer first thing in the morning. I know—like that will help.

The bottom line is I have three choices regarding Kanook, all of which suck, pardon my French:

1. I 'send the dog away' the way I did with Doogie, and although that's what I'd most like to do, I'm not especially keen on getting arrested again. Kanook's condition, although life-threatening without proper treatment and in the wrong hands, is not immediately dire, especially since I've been getting some food into him with the enzymes and he already looks better after five days with me. He's not at death's door this second.

2. Give him back to her, with a better agreement in place saying she'll take him to the vet and get the test done, and that she'll buy him the proper food if he turns out to have the disease. Since she's already backed out on the first agreement, I believe this option is too risky for the dog's sake. She can't be trusted to do what is right for him on her own. She could totally starve this dog in a matter of weeks given his current condition, and her unwillingness to buy him the enzymes for his food makes me know she doesn't take his health seriously.

3. Get in cahoots with the humane officer. Given that he screwed me in the Doogie case and lied on the witness stand at my trial, I'm not eager to work with him again on anything. But he's my only legal chance at getting this woman convicted of cruelty or getting her to give the dog up. It's not a good one.

I leave Officer G. a message on both the office phone and his super-secret-police-phone-that-he-always-answers-except-when-I'm-calling-him-as-he-told-me-to-about-Doogie. I ask him to call me ASAP as I have a case I really need to speak to him about today because the owner wants the dog back and I believe it's a cruelty case.

To his credit he calls me back very quickly; I don't think he's eager to repeat the Doogie incident, or maybe he actually has some guilt over his behavior...nah. That would be wishful thinking.

I explain the story to him, and he offers to meet me and Kanook at Sheetz around 10 a.m. He says he will check over Kanook, and then we'll go to her house to see if we can resolve the issue.

Shortly after I arrange a meeting with Officer G., Dragon Lady calls and states again that she wants Kanook back. I ask her if she is willing to pay for the enzymes that Dogs Deserve Better bought for him.

She refuses, saying she is going to start him on the bones and fat she got from the butcher. I tell her to call me when she gets home at 3:00 p.m.

I drive Kanook to meet the officer, but I hate every second of it. I know in my gut it's Kanook who will pay the price.

Officer G. looks the dog over, asking me if he's friendly before approaching him...I guess he's seen his fair share of aggressive dogs, too.

He decides his condition is a 3. That's only one step below ideal body condition! I disagree with that analysis, although I know his condition has improved in the days since I had him in my care. Still, even 30 lbs. underweight would surely be a 2, not a 3.

He agrees that she has to either get the dog vet care, or give up the dog. The best news is that he promises me if she gives up the dog, he will give Kanook back to me! Fingers crossed for Kanook. A spark of hope ignites.

We drive to her house; she isn't home, but the three min pins are out in the kennel on the porch. Officer G. knocks on the door, then goes around to the back to knock. He tells us there are more dogs inside, and asks me if she's breeding.

I say, "I know she's breeding min pins, because every so often she puts up a sign saying min pins for sale," and he says she's got puppies in there right now.

He thinks it will be best if I sign Kanook over to him, and then he can force her to play ball with him.

I hate it, and I'm sad. I love the dog. But it's his only hope.

I sign over Kanook to him on the same poorly-written agreement she and I had created on the vet records from his previous caretaker.

Dragon Lady had no vet records of her own.

I discuss Kanook's food situation with the humane officer, and he tells us we can bring some enzymes down to the shelter for them to mix with his food. It may take a couple of days for him to figure out what will happen with the dog. Poor Skells. Stuck in a shelter after knowing love, sleeping in a warm house, and finally believing his life will get better.

Shortly after I get home, Dragon Lady calls and asks me what's going on. I tell her I gave Kanook to the humane officer, that I gave her every chance to work with us, but if she was going to threaten me with police action and go back on her side of the bargain, then I was bringing in the authorities myself.

She says, "Good, do you still have that agreement form, because I want to turn that over to my attorney."

Yeah, I'll get right on that...Oh, that's right, I gave it to the humane officer when I signed over the dog to him.

She asks, sounding maybe a teensy bit intimidated at this point, "What's he gonna' do?"

I tell her I assume he's going to cite her for cruelty to animals. (But do I really believe it? No.)

Then, and here's the gem, she tells me "Why, I told you why he was so skinny."

I say, "Really, now why was that?"

She flounders about a bit and then says, "It was because I ran out of deer meat."

So when he wasn't eating your leftover deer carcasses, his only option was to starve to death? Look Dragon Lady, either you were starving him, or he has worms or other physical problems you're not addressing. It's that simple.

I tell her to take it up with the humane officer, and hang up.

Heather and I mix up some lunch for Kanook with his enzymes, and Heather drops it off along with a three day supply of enzymes. I later call her to see what happened at the shelter.

She tells me that they were not to nice to her there, and they had already fed him hamburger and rice! Two things he shouldn't have anyway if he has EPI, and without enzymes! I just want to cry. Now my hard work to get his stool normal might go down the drain, along with whatever progress he has made in five days with me.

I wait the rest of the day, thinking of him in that freaking shelter, and don't hear back from Officer G. I'll be calling him first thing in the morning to find out if she came to take poor Kanook back. I will probably drive by there in the morning, but it will kill me if I see him out in that pen.

Chapter 11

YOU ARE NOT PERFECT:
LETTING GO OF MISTAKES

Levi on his chain. Note how he isn't even paying attention to his rescuers...
he's too busy looking at the house to see if his guardians will give him a
scrap of attention, even though they've treated him so poorly. Luckily for
him, his was a rescue that didn't go wrong. DDB rescued him, I fostered
him, and he got a wonderful inside home and family.

Truth: You are not perfect, and neither are all the 'perfect' rescuers. Everyone, everyone, EVERYONE makes mistakes, and to expect perfection of yourself or anyone else will only make your life miserable.

Tip: Fostering dogs is hard. Expecting yourself to do it perfectly, be the perfect foster parent will only make it worse, so let go of this need. The rescue world is rife with judgment surrounding foster parenting. If others condemn you as not good enough, walk away from them and keep doing your best.

Repeat after me: I'm doing my best, and getting it done is more important than getting it perfect. I am taking the best care of my fosters that I can, and letting go of my mistakes.

ॐ

I would prefer to keep excessive negativity out of this book—as in talking bad about other rescuers—because I think we all get enough of that in our daily lives. This book is aimed at forgiving yourself (and others) for true mistakes, learning how to do it better, and giving yourself the time and attention you need too.

However, at this point I must say a few words about the cruelty and vindictiveness that runs rampant in the rescue community.

It's bullshit.

Too many rescuers think that every other rescuer is not as good as they are for all manner of reasons. I've been slammed by people for not being perfect enough, not doing this right, not doing that right.

It's exhausting!

In just one example of the myriad out there, one person who thought she could do it so much better than me had a house full of dogs—eight, if I'm not mistaken (she had a problem letting the dogs go once they crossed her threshold). I know for a fact—having seen it with my own eyes—that her dogs spent their entire lives either trapped in the kitchen, in a crate, or in a tiny 10x20 yard.

They never went for walks; she claimed they didn't need them.

Were these dogs chained or penned, no. Did they live inside, yes. Was she clean, yes, she seemed to be. Would I have badmouthed her efforts, even though I didn't think it was ideal?

No. It is my opinion that her dogs did not have the best life available to them, and she should have let some go. But, at the same time, I believed that she loved them and had good intentions. I accepted that her standards were not mine and keep my eyes focused on the real and true abusers out there.

By contrast, at that time I had two separate large fenced areas (approximately 1/2 acre total), two doggie doors, the ability to separate dogs into packs so they could roam free inside the home, and a super-sized crate plus smaller crates for use when absolutely necessary. They were rarely used once dogs got acclimated.

I learned this person had been judging my rescue and foster efforts and finding them wanting. Why?

Because she believes she's the perfect rescuer. Perfect foster parent. She is unable to see the log in her own eye for the splinter in mine.

Another time I was accused of being a bad rescuer because I adopted a dog into a home where, a year later, he was alleged to have been hit by the male caretaker. The informant was his sister. Turns out that, coincidentally, they were involved in a family brawl over their mother's death and her will, and weren't speaking to each other.

Sammy, the 'abused' dog, in his yard, looking happy and healthy.

The dog, Sammy, and I became mere pawns in their family game of pain.

In order to disprove the internet rumors, I made the decision to take a whole Saturday, make the two hour drive to the dog's home, and take photos and video of what appeared to be a happy and well-adjusted dog.

Was the guy taking a swat at the dog on occasion? Maybe, maybe not. I saw no signs of it. I had no proof, just unsubstantiated allegations; the dog appeared in good health, happy, and well-loved. He showed no fear of his caretakers, and he was just as sweet and loving as the day I adopted him out.

To you good folks out there who are so discouraged with fostering and rescue because of the meanness of other rescuers, I feel your pain.

If you know in your heart you are kind and doing your best for your foster dogs, then block the person from your life. Delete their e-mail, ban them from contacting you through social media, whatever you have to do so you don't see their abuse every day. You don't need that stress.

However, I will encourage you to do as I did with Sammy and take the time to first rebut the lies. Take photos and video of the dog/s in question, and post all your evidence that disproves the allegations. Don't get me wrong—they will still badmouth you and disbelieve you—but they will lose a lot of support when others see your photos and video. They say a picture is worth 1,000 words, and I've found that to be true.

After I took photos and video of Sammy happily playing in the stream with the family's other dog, and running in and out the doggie door, people moved on to the next person to attack with their pitchforks and computer mouses.

Honestly, to those of you who spend your lives torturing other rescuers, get off it! Keep your eyes focused on the true abusers. Leave your fellow rescuers alone, unless you see real problems such as hoarding, chaining, 24/7 crating, or lack of medical attention. These things need to be taken seriously.

If you really believe a fellow rescuer is abusing their animals, you'd better get proof, and you'd better be prepared to step in to take the dogs off their hands so the dogs don't pay the price by ending up dumped and killed in the shelter.

Otherwise, keep your head in the game and focus on the 'real' bad guys...

Foster Diary: I wake up to no Banshee in the bedroom for the second day. He does come to see me, but he's very lethargic, and I see puke on his face again. I thought he would be better by this morning, so now I'm really getting worried; his health is getting worse instead of better. I call the vet to find out what to do.

The vet assistant tells me that if he threw up three times the first night he should have gotten most of it out of his system; there isn't much we can do but wait and see.

But that doesn't feel like enough. I feel bad for him, and I worry that he could have damaged his liver or something. It's good that he's up and walking around, I think to myself. Maybe he'll be ok?

In six years I've never had a dog take a bottle off that counter, although they have taken food from wherever they can sniff it out. But they're dogs, and formerly-chained dogs without training, so that's to be expected.

The ibuprofen should have been shut inside the box where I keep my other over-the-counter meds; time and laziness and other dogs not bothering with stuff made me sloppy. I feel horribly guilty, and it sucks.

At 9:30 a.m. I call the humane officer, and he actually answers his super-secret cell phone, there's a first! I ask him if there's any news on Kanook, and he says that Dragon Lady called him yesterday, and he's waiting to see if she provides him with proof of license and rabies.

He called the vet in Ebensburg to see if he did the test for the Exocrine Pancreatic Insufficiency, and he did not. The vet wants to see the dog this week or next again to give him the test unless he's gained weight.

Dragon Lady will be forced to take the dog back to this vet or to another vet for a follow-up visit, and to provide proof of that to the humane officer. She also is accruing daily fees by leaving Kanook at the Humane Society. He repeated that he will give the dog over to us if she releases him.

He tells me that technically right now he cannot keep Kanook as a cruelty case because Pennsylvania's laws don't give him enough power. I think that's a load of crap.

I ask him how long he thinks it would take him to die being that skinny, because he seems like a skeleton to me, and I just can't imagine that isn't cruelty. He says he agrees with me, and there's no way in Hell that Dragon Lady should get the dog back after letting him get into the shape he is in.

But that's just words, and they mean nothing. Apparently she will get Kanook back because he won't fight for the dog's rights.

Nice. That's exactly what I expected would happen. Between Kanook and Banshee, I'm not having a good day.

❦

We decide to take Banshee into the vet anyway after he pukes up his breakfast again. There he gets a Vitamin K shot and pills to coat his stomach and intestines. He is still lethargic and not like himself at all; he won't even look at food.

Towards evening it occurs to me that maybe he ingested some of the plastic bottle, and it's stuck in his colon causing problems. We're going back to the vet in the morning.

Chapter 12

THE DOGS LOVE YOU ANYWAY: THEY DON'T CARE IF YOU'RE PERFECT

℘

Rosie Bearito was one of my early fosters, and she loved me no matter what. Your fosters will love you too! She was found in West Virginia, running down the road dragging her chain. We got so attached that she became my son's dog, and he loved her so much he even cleaned up her 'walk-n-poops.' What's a 'walk-n-poop', you ask? Well, Rosie didn't want to go outside, so she'd hold it as long as she could, and then she'd run for the doggie door, with poop flying out her butt all the way. Rosie started my love affair with akitas, who are a very cool breed.

Truth: Dogs don't care how perfect or imperfect you are, how clean your house is, how much money you have, or anything else. What they do care about is being with you; the more they can be with you, the happier they are.

Tip: No matter how many times you screw up, the dogs still love you. Seek to improve their conditions and treatment, yes, but remember they love you just because you love them.

Repeat after me: My foster dogs are well-cared for and grateful that I'm giving them a chance at a better life; they love me for trying my best, even when I make mistakes.

❦

No more negativity allowed; I've said my piece with that, so for now, let's focus on YOU.

First, let's do an honest assessment of your fostering situation and your home environment:

Are you doing your best for your foster dogs, and even if you can't reach your best every day, are you consistent in your care?

Do they have food, water, a soft bed, love, and exercise?

Do you take them to the vet, get them spayed/neutered, and wormed?

Then you're doing great! I adore you, and thank you on behalf of the dogs and those who've been there and know how hard it is!

Really, and think about it, can you be such a bad person if you're trying this hard?

No more judging yourself, getting down on yourself, or living by how others judge you. Sometimes you screw up, the way I've done with Banshee. I have to forgive myself, and so do you.

When you are feeling anxious about your ability to keep trying for the dogs, take a deep breath, accept your feelings, and then let them go. Decide instead to feel joy and love, and picture you and your foster dog encompassed in joy and love.

Wow, doesn't that feel better?

Foster Diary: Banshee is not looking good this morning; when I get up he's laying on the porch. He never lays on the porch. He had thrown up his first pill from the vet last evening. He stands and drinks water, but is wobbly, and his ribs are starting to show from three days without any food staying down.

Now I'm really scared. I call the vet again, and take him up at 10:00 a.m. I'm supposed to be getting the DDB calendar ready for the printer this week, and it has to be at press by Friday; but neither Kim nor Heather are working.

It falls to me, and I know his life is much more important than the calendar. I'll have to work late tonight, that's all.

I ask the vet to take an X-ray of his colon to see if there is anything blocking his intestines. Turns out he's full of excrement, which shouldn't be happening since he hasn't had any nutrition make its way through in days. The vet does bloodwork and gives him an enema. The bloodwork won't be back for a day, but the enema starts to work right away, and they direct me out by the dumpsters to see how things emerge.

He's really struggling to get the first download out, and

I am hunkered down, watching to see if there's a bottle cap or anything of that nature coming out. I can't help but think what a funny picture I must make to passers-by, scrutinizing a dog taking a dump, but that's how it is in the dog world—you do what you gotta' do when you gotta' do it. Right?

So he finally passes a log, and short of digging through it, it seems to be normal—I see no protuberances which would lead me to believe he ingested any plastic. However, it is large and very impacted, so hopefully getting things moving might be a step in a positive direction for him.

On the way home I stop off at the store to buy more supplies—dog and cat food and paper towels. I have to drive with the windows down because the downloading continued while I was in the store, and the van smells like a barnyard.

I ask him how he's doing, and his big brown eyes still look at me with love. I send up a prayer that he will pull through this ok, and I start making that deal with God, you know the one; I promise never to leave ANYTHING on the counter ever again, God, if only Banshee can just pull through this one time...please? I swear!

❧

When I get home I look for a message from Officer G. about Kanook, but there's nothing there. I had driven by her house, and saw the min pins out in the pen, but there was no sign of Kanook. Either she didn't get him back, or she has him hidden away in the house.

The phone rings, and after the call I immediately search for

Banshee to see how he's doing. He's laying downstairs with his head on the water dish; blood is dripping out his butt.

Oh, God! Now I'm panicking.

I call the vet again, and they tell me to bring him back up. I'm terrified that he's going to die, angry at myself, angry at Heather, and angry at the vet for not doing more from the start on Monday morning. Because of our collective dismissals and inadequacies, Banshee may pay with his life.

They come out to the van, give him another shot and give me additional meds to get into him every six hours. I bring him home, and he just lays there. He's cold, and I worry that he's in shock. My daughter Brynnan is crying her little eyes out. I ask her to help me send him good thoughts so he can get better. I know we aren't making things better by sitting around crying and whining; we have to think positive and send him good energy. It's gonna be a long night.

Chapter 13

FOSTER JUST ONE MORE: STRETCHING YOUR BOUNDARIES

⅋

Adio was released to DDB, and when I picked him up to foster him I saw he was chained to a doghouse I recognized from a previous rescue. They'd just given it to another family member! From this we learned to take the doghouse with us when we freed the dog. If they don't have the 'tools' readily available to chain a dog, maybe they will think twice about doing it. When I went back to get the doghouse, Adio's former owner threatened to shoot me! It was my first and last direct death threat.

Truth: When it comes to fostering, there are two kinds of dog lovers: those who don't foster enough or at all and those who foster too many. We need to find that happy medium.

Tip: For those of you with 100 excuses why you can't foster, or can't foster more than one in your lifetime, cover your mouth, jump in with both feet, and foster just one more.

Repeat after me: I can stretch myself and commit to foster one more dog. Then I'll use my Get Out of Fostering Free Card.

❧

I know what you're thinking. After reading about the difficulties of fostering, the heartaches you endure, and all the nastiness you put up with from other rescuers, you're saying to yourself "Why the heck would I EVER foster another dog as long as I live?"

Yeah. That is a good question.

I wonder that too.

But remember, we don't foster for ourselves, or even for other people. We foster for the dogs, to give them a decent, soft place to land while they recuperate from abuse, from chaining, from abandonment, or from a shelter situation.

We are their halfway houses. We give them more than they had and less than they will gain in their wonderful, forever home.

If everyone who fostered only one time in their life, or fosters only one dog at a time, stretches themselves just a little more and fosters just that one more dog, there will be thousands more who get help each year.

During my years with DDB, I had many area reps who didn't foster, at all, and even though we didn't reject them for not fostering, it was my personal belief that every rep should foster at least one dog at least one time. After all, how can we expect others to foster for us if we're refusing to lead by example?

I get a kick out of people who would call me for help for a chained dog, and then say, "Well, the neighbor might let me have the dog, but then what would I do with him? I can't keep him here, because I already have a dog." And, like an idiot, I would take that excuse as a damn fine one, and rapidly flail about searching for a foster home for that dog. Which usually ended up being me.

Duh.

If you're that stressed about a dog near you, and by some wonderful miracle you are able to get that dog off the chain, pipe down and foster the dog already! I know you can do it. After all, who would be more ecstatic about that dog being off the chain than you? (And the dog, of course! But that's why you're so happy...because you don't have to watch him/her suffer anymore.)

I do understand that you'd be a tad bit inconvenienced... but so would I be if I dropped everything, ran over to your house, picked up your neighbor's unneutered-chained-monster-of-a-male dog, and brought him home to urinate all over my house and hump all my other foster dogs.

Just sayin'...

Everyone's gotta do their share.

Foster Diary: I get up early to check on Banshee. He's incredibly lethargic, cold, and I'm sure he's in shock. He can't even get up now.

I try to remain calm, but inside I'm truly freaking out, and I call a different vet to ask if we can bring Banshee in as an emergency. I know if he has any chance at all he's got to be hospitalized immediately. He's made it through the night, but I know now that things are really bad.

I give her the details of his case, and she tells me to bring him at 9:00 a.m.

Kim drives him up, and the vet tells her what I already know in my heart; he might not make it. His kidneys have failed. We screwed up.

They say he should have been at the emergency vet on Sunday when we thought he first ingested the pills, and now he may die; how will I live with the guilt?

Poor Banshee.

I guess it's not my day for foster successes. Officer G. calls to tell me that Dragon Lady took poor Kanook back, and so far is complying with him.

I hope it costs her money, at least.

He is forcing her to take him to the vet within the week for a followup visit. If she doesn't comply, he tells me he will arrest her and seize the dog. I think he's just telling me what I want to hear to get me off his back.

I can't help but feel like I've let two dogs down this week, and it's not a good feeling.

I'm crying off and on, although sometimes I feel like my emotions are stuffed inside me. I can't eat, which is rare and I should stick with that feeling. Maybe I'd be skinny. I can't help the intense feelings of horror and guilt about the potential loss of Banshee because of mistakes by me, my staff, and by the first vet's office.

As far as Kanook's circumstances go, it went as I fully expected it would by turning him over to the humane officer. His right to a decent life is all but nonexistent.

I know I'm human, and I have to forgive myself, but I wonder how I can do that. I'm in the business of saving lives, and now one may be gone forever, and one has gone back to a negligent caretaker because I 'did the right thing.'

According to the law, of course.

But what is right 'according to the law' is often not what is morally right, and Kanook may end up paying the price with his life too. In my opinion, God's laws protect animals, and man's laws protect abusers.

And it's raining, which is just perfect.

❧

About 6:30 p.m., the vet calls with some guardedly good news...Banshee peed! This is excellent news when you're facing kidney failure, because if the kidneys are completely shut down the dog won't be able to make urine.

He's not out of the woods yet, by any means, but if his kidneys start working again he can bounce back.

I'm so happy! I have regained a sense of hope. I call Kim and Heather to tell them the good news.

I didn't realize how much Banshee livened up the house! It seems so quiet without him. I complained that he drove me crazy, but now I'm literally bereft without him here. Huh.

Chapter 14

FOSTER JUST ONE LESS: FINDING SOME BOUNDARIES

℘

Bridget, the blind akita on the left, was one of the many akitas I fostered. Photos like this remind us why we do this work. Bridget had a whole lot of love come her way with her new family, and that made any training issues I went through with her seem immaterial. She more than deserved her own happy ending, and I was blessed to be able to provide that for her by fostering her and letting her go to her perfect situation.

Truth: There are those of us out there, including myself, who have to learn to say and mean the word NO. While the need is certainly great, we cannot do it all ourselves.

Tip: If you're psychologically struggling with eight dogs in your house, and you know that you can better handle six, make a vow to yourself and everyone around you that you will say NO until you get three dogs adopted...at which time you say yes to only ONE. Get it?

Repeat after Me: No, no, no, no, no, no, no....you get the picture.

⸎

I know most of you reading this book are probably like I was for years...you have a hard time saying NO, letting dogs down, letting people down, looking like you're not doing a good job, or like you're not a good person.

But, even IF you said YES to every single dog that came your way looking for a foster home, trust me, you'd do it forever and never be done.

One year Dogs Deserve Better tried to do just that. We were saying YES to every dog we could handle (or THOUGHT we could handle), and they were coming in droves. We spent over $100,000 in vet care, but nothing stemmed the flow.

Instead, we succeeded in making ourselves miserable and destroying our area rep program by letting in irresponsible people who only made us look bad. It was a brutal lesson.

So you have to find some boundaries for yourself. If being Super-Saving-Dog-Woman will not make it go away, then why are you killing yourself? Because trust me, for the naysayers and the never-ending line of dogs in trouble, it will never be enough, no matter what you do...

I swear to you, if I knew for a fact that if we each fostered five additional dogs this year that the rescue crisis would be over, I'd be the first to say "Let's do it!"

I could suck it up for another year.

But it won't. The need will stay the same as long as our addiction to being needed remains in place...never-ending.

So now you, theoretically, have a house full of dogs and you're miserable. You feel like you have no life of your own, no happiness, everything revolves around the needs of these dogs and getting through each day caring for them.

The need to feel needed, to feel important, to fill the gaping hole in our gut or our heart is psychological, and many of us come into this world with it or we develop it early in life due to our environmental stressors.

Some people fill the hole with shopping, some with sex. Some with food.

Some of us fill ours with rescue. (And then maybe shopping, sex, and food.) My subconscious belief has been that rescuing the next critter will somehow save my soul, make me feel good about myself, earn me a spot in heaven. I don't wish to speak for you, but I suspect I'm not alone in this.

And it does make you feel good, temporarily. I feel great when I take a dog off a chain, and then see him/her snuggled up safe and warm on a doggie bed beside my desk. How could that not feel awesome?

It IS a great experience, and you DESERVE to feel great for doing it.

It just can't be another addiction.

An addiction to rescuing dogs you can't possibly care for.

Soon it's just another mouth to feed, another dog to train, another needy soul sucking your life energy away. There's no time for you, because—guess what—you planned it that way; you planned, subconsciously, to fill your life with taking care of others so you didn't have to think about what would REALLY make you happy.

But you're not happy. And though you're overwhelmed and giving 200%, there's still just as much need out there as ever. You're putting your finger in a tiny dam hole; sooner or later it overflows the top or bursts the entire structure.

So it's time to say NO. Trust me, I'm with you. I'm saying NO more and more these days, and so are you. Yes, there is always a temporary wave of guilt, but in the end it's better, because you aren't putting yourself last anymore. And guess what? Without scapegoats to pile all the work on, others will start to step up and do their share. We must stop enabling them by swooping in and causing ourselves further harm.

Determine your absolute limit of fosters that you can handle without feeling overburdened, and that would give you time to work on YOU, find an activity that you enjoy.

What's your number?

Now, no matter what, you will no longer exceed that limit, unless it's just an overnight. Are you with me?

Foster Diary: Right now I've got only five dogs here, but I'm riddled with guilt and worry about Banshee, and so heartbroken over Kanook.

Luckily, though, the other dogs in the house are mellow, so taking care of them during this stressful time is a piece of cake.

The vet calls around 10:30 a.m. to say that Banshee's blood numbers are a little better, but they are changing his fluids to add more electrolytes because his potassium and other readings are still off. He is peeing, so they are encouraged.

They say I can come visit him anytime before 5:00 p.m.

‍ ❧

I haven't been to this vet's office in awhile. They are incredibly nice people and good vets; however, they won't give us a rescue discount, and that's so hard on a nonprofit.

We don't use them nearly as often as we'd like for financial reasons; mostly in tough cases, emergencies, or life and death situations.

Vets really need to donate some services to nonprofits. I understand putting a limit on it, or even just giving a 10% discount to 501c3s. But nothing? No budging? That makes me wonder why you are in the business. Help those who are helping the needy by donating a portion of your work, even a small one.

When I arrive to visit him, they still remember me, calling me by name. The vet takes me back to see Banshee. He's in a small raised cage, and he doesn't even acknowledge me at first. That scares me, but when the doctor opens the door and I start to talk to him, he lifts his head to see 'his mommy,' and it's higher than he was able to lift it the day before.

Yay! Hope!

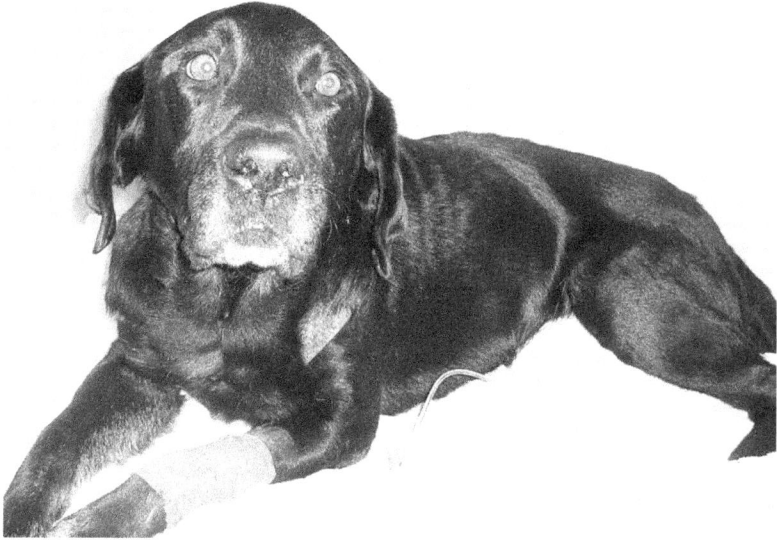

His eyes look at me like, "Hi, Mom, did you come to spring me?"

I smile at him, caress him, massage his head, tell him how much I love him. He stinks to high heaven, and I can see pee on the blanket under him; it's yellow, which I think is a good sign his kidneys are working.

The poor guy hasn't kept any food down since Sunday, but the vet is happy that he hasn't thrown up since being hospitalized. I stay with him for 15 minutes, telling him over and over again that I'm sorry and I love him, and the vet promises to call on Saturday with an update.

They aren't open to visitors on the weekends, which stinks because my daughter Brynnan would really love to see him, and seeing us again would cheer Banshee up. He was a different dog when I was there, more alive.

I feel so happy and so hopeful that he's going to live now. It's like Christmas came early!

Chapter 15

PUT BOUNDARIES IN PLACE: DECIDING WHAT YOU CAN AND CAN'T LIVE WITH

⅋

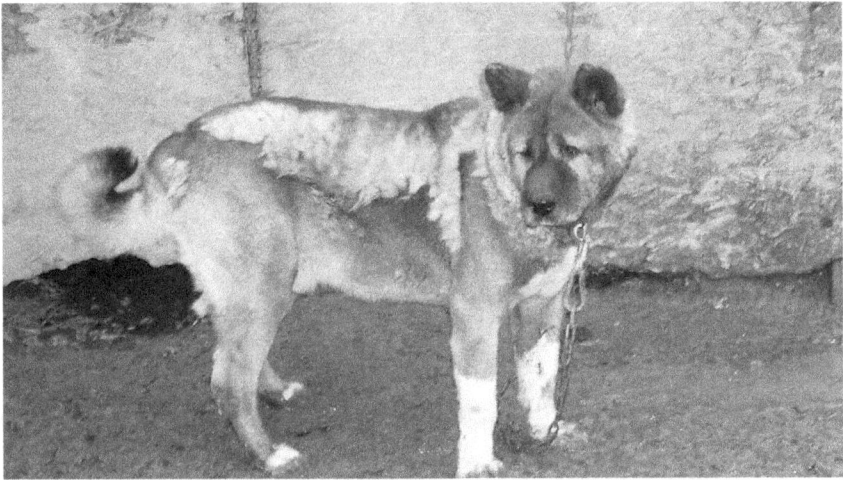

Mojo lived in about the worst conditions imaginable for a chained dog. His world consisted of a mud hole at the front of a trailer, with a decrepit doghouse, and not a bit of dry land to lay his head. Note all the clumps of fur all over him. Akitas 'blow coat,' and loving caretakers take steps to remove the fur (which is kinda' fun.) His guardians could have cared less.

Truth: It's easy to know you should say NO, but harder to implement boundaries and stick with your convictions when faced with a needy dog. You may have to stop putting yourself in the position where you are tempted to say YES when you need to say NO. It's like an alcoholic avoiding the bars.

Tip: Figure out what triggers you to say YES when you should say NO, and avoid that trigger. Keep your NO firmly in your mind, no matter what. Know you already have a house full of fosters; you are already doing your share. Others must step up to help.

Repeat after me: I am full, I am full, I am full, I am full. (Hold hands over ears and eyes.) La-la-la la-la-la.

⚮

Most of us who need to put boundaries in place against taking in more dogs than we can handle have a trigger that tempts us to say YES when we need to say NO. I know what mine always was when I was with DDB: Social media! E-mail with pictures! Personally-addressed e-mails!

How many requests through social media or e-mails do you get in a single day with pleas to help dogs in need?

I used to get about 30 e-mails every day asking for my or the organization's help with a certain chained dog. Even if I said YES to only one dog a day, in a week I'd have seven more dogs! Can you see the dilemma? There's no way I'm adopting out seven dogs in one week, every week! Plus getting them the vet care and training they need? Not happening.

We had to disable the ability for people to message us through our Facebook page, because once we started climbing to near a million fans, there was no way we could funnel all the requests for help. We had to force them to come through our e-mail channels so they could be addressed, and we could point out all the options for helping chained dogs.

I finally changed my e-mail address, and tasked DDB employees with answering e-mails from the old address and passing along requests for help to area reps or putting pleas out through our social media for local rescuers.

This helped tremendously...I still had way too many foster dogs, but not so much guilt.

As DDB grew larger, my travel requirements grew accordingly. I traveled to speak at least one weekend a month, and this was not something that was negotiable as far as I was concerned. It was my job to be out there meeting people and educating at every opportunity if I wanted to help ALL chained dogs rather than the few. I realized I must cut my fostering down even more to make sure everyone got the care they require while I was gone, and remained safe.

If you are overwhelmed, come up with a similar plan. Cut out the groups that take up too much of your time with little return. Limit your social media engagement, unsubscribe from at least half the groups you've somehow become a member of. Stick to those groups that make you feel good about yourself, encouraged, where you feel most motivated to do the most good.

Simplify!

I suggest that instead of helping three nonprofits, choose one to help for this year. Each year, choose again or affirm your commitment to your current organization, and so on and so forth. You will feel less overwhelmed and see more progress because your efforts are more focused and your joy will be tripled. You will feel more appreciated and more involved, and your energy will not be split all over the place.

Foster Diary: The vet calls bright and early, well, 9:00 a.m., to tell me some encouraging news about Banshee. Banshee sat up when he came into the room, was alert, peed, and let loose on some major diarrhea when he walked him outside.

In fact, he almost pulled the vet's arm off when he took him outside to use the bathroom. That's my crazy boy! The vet was very encouraged, and for the first time said he believed Banshee was out of the woods.

I'm ecstatic, and doing the happy dance!

Mid-morning a former adopter calls, this time it's Nala's 'mother.' They are losing their house and she wonders if I can take Nala back. The mortgage crisis affects rescues just as severely or moreso than anyone else, because not only has funding for our efforts slipped, but more and more dogs are coming back from decent homes due to loss of the abode.

I try to accommodate returned dogs whenever I possibly can. Since I've committed to the dog, I can't in good conscience allow him/her to be thrown in a shelter. In this case I'll make room, because I know Nala and care about her greatly. There's no way in Hell I'm leaving her to a bad situation.

I'm not happy about it, but the woman is crying and I soften. I get angry because we bear the brunt of people's financial hardships at a time when these hardships are rolling down onto me personally as well as onto the organization.

But I am not in her shoes; I am not faced with losing everything, so I keep my mouth shut and schedule a pick up for later.

❧

I drive by Dragon Lady's house to see if I can catch a glimpse of Kanook on the way to the library, where my daughter Brynnan and I are going for a miniature doll house class, a mother-daughter bonding activity.

I'm driving slowly so I can see if he's out in the pen, but I don't see him. I DO see her standing there watching me, though. At least I annoy her.

❧

When I pick up Nala later, I see she's gotten even fatter! Hounds are known for a tendency to thicken about the middle, and every hound I've fostered has expanded exponentially, but this girl only seems to get wider with time.

She looks healthy enough otherwise, and it appears they've taken decent care of her. It could have been a lot worse.

There's a little blond-haired girl standing beside the kitchen table, probably just six years old. She's looking down, emotionally cutting herself off from the pain. I surmise that she's devastated to be losing her dog, maybe her best friend. Her mom is crying, and the little girl just stands there, stoney-faced, trying not to let her distress show, to expose her.

I feel uncomfortable because I'm an unwilling witness to their private suffering. The little girl hands me a note she wrote to Nala, telling her she loves her and she'll miss her. Gah, now I want to cry too.

I remember how much my pets meant to me when I was a child, even though they were not allowed in the house. I spent countless hours in the barn with my kitties, especially my brown tabby cat, Streaker. I'd curl up in the hay with her, and we'd cuddle for hours. Streaker was shy, and I was the only one she'd allow to pet her, so I was very protective of her.

I felt Streaker was all I had, my only loving bond, and then one day she was gone, along with four of our five other cats. Turned out my father had killed all the cats but one because my mother complained about them wanting to come in the house all the time.

The little girl's pain brings back my own memories of suffering over the loss of my animal friends at a young age. I have more in common with the her than I realized.

Nala obviously remembers me; she's happy to see me and I'm happy to see her too. Welcome home, Nala. I'll do better next time! (Why do I feel like I say that a lot?)

Chapter 16

KNOW WHEN TO SAY NO: STICKING TO YOUR BOUNDARIES

&

Sess was one of my first rescues, and he showed an amazing loyalty and devotion to me. Sess was rescued from a pen out west, and transported all the way to DDB in Pennsylvania. He was old when I started fostering him, and I fell so in love with him that he stayed with me until he passed. I wish I had a lifetime with this special dog, and knowing that his former guardians wasted his God-given faithfulness by throwing him outside and leaving him alone really frosted my pumpkin.

Truth: There's no cut and dried answer as to when to keep a firm NO in place. But, if you're feeling overwhelmed by your home situation, that's a major clue that the time is NOW.

Tip: You don't need to have an earth-shattering excuse for saying NO. You can simply say "I'm not able to foster another dog right now," and others will respect that. No need to flail about.

Repeat after me: I know I'm doing all I can do; I understand my boundaries, and I will no longer overwhelm myself. I already have [fill in the blank] fosters, and I am at my limit.

❦

I know it's easier said than done, to just say NO, regardless of circumstances, especially when it's a returned dog. I was at capacity when both Sweet Pea and Nala came back. But there was no part of me that would have allowed those two sweet dogs to end up in the shelter, so I took them back, and don't regret it.

I knew both dogs, and they were well-behaved, easy dogs. I also knew I would not have to housetrain them, people train them, or obedience train them. They knew my house, and they were able to fit smoothly and easily back into the daily routine, without a fuss and without fights or squabbles with the other foster dogs.

But I would not have taken another foster into my home at that point if there was ANY other possible solution. A new dog, directly off the chain or out of a pen, would have caused more turmoil than I would have been able to handle.

I recommend when looking for help for a dog near you, that you put major effort into finding another foster home if you are at capacity. Don't make the mistake of thinking you're the only possible solution for this dog.

Open your horizons and believe that people will step up.

When I was actively rescuing, if I put enough effort into finding another foster home, I often succeeded; if not I'd look long enough that I ended up with an adoption for one of my fosters, at which point I had the space to take the dog into my home.

Here's my procedure if you'd like to make use of it. I still do this today when I get involved with local rescue efforts, and it is very effective. This is for chained or penned dog rescue, but it can be adapted to about any rescue situation, including home or shelter.

I get off my butt (the hardest part, but the most crucial!), and drive to where the dog is located to ensure the dog care-takers are really willing to give up the dog. In my line of rescue the dog is always outside the home somewhere, either on the chain or in a pen, and I want to see the conditions. I tell the people who want to give up the dog that I need the photos in order to find a foster home and for my records, both of which are true.

Meeting the dog is crucial to ascertain the level of chain-aggression, and to get a feel for how easy the dog will be to assimilate into a foster home.

I take a ton of photos, because even after all this time and direct knowledge of the kind of photos that work best—eye-level, being sure to see the chain and the doghouse in the photo too—I still take 10 bad photos for every good one. I can't tell you how many times I've ended up with no decent photos even when I think I have some—so take lots.

I choose the three best photos, downsize them to 72 dpi at 12 inches wide, add the dog's sad story, and start crossposting them around the internet via social media. Typically the first go-round gets no whispers of help.

I used to stop there, throw my hands up, and take the dog into my home, pitying myself and wondering why I couldn't get any help. But I eventually learned that was the wrong approach, and I had to trust the universe to provide.

Two days later I send out a second plea, leaving everything else much the same as before, except that I add "Second Plea" to the headline.

Usually it takes a third plea to see some action. By then someone who has room or has made room will come along and offer to take the dog in.

There ARE solutions out there that aren't you. Do your share, do your best, and trust that others will come along and take up the slack that you can't handle. You don't have to be Super-Saving-Dog-Woman (or Man)!

Foster Diary: While I'm out running errands, the vet calls, leaving a message that Banshee is MUCH improved this morning, and should come home tomorrow.

You can't imagine the relief! What a load off—I have doggy-proofed my counters in preparation for his homecoming, and I solemnly swear to keep all meds, even over-the-counter meds, safely out of his reach and the reach of subsequent foster dogs, as promised to the gods in my bargaining session.

I'm on my way back from picking my son up at a friend's

around 8:00 p.m., when I see a critter up ahead in the forest-ed darkness. I slow down, only to realize it's a smallish dog, and there are no houses nearby.

Crap! Why can't it be a possum, a raccoon, or a skunk?

There's garbage sitting along the side of the road, and he's investigating it. I stop, and he comes near but not up to me. He appears to be a terrier-kinda dog, white with black patches, short-haired, medium-sized. He growls a bit when I get too near, but I can tell it's just fear. He's wary.

He keeps running around the van like he wants to get in, but he won't let me touch him. I try opening the back, since I know it works for my dogs, and—for better or worse—he jumps right in.

He's obviously familiar with riding in the car and enjoys it. I tell myself that maybe he's just lost, and someone will be looking for him come morning.

He has a ring on his neck where the fur is flattened from collar-wear, but there's no collar, and I hope he hasn't slipped his chain . . . that's all I need. By the time I get home and out to the van with a leash, he has somehow wiggled his way up to the front. I am able to easily noose him and bring him inside.

The dogs upstairs are barking, so he doesn't want to come in, and poops on the floor in his nervousness. He's downstairs with Nala, but he can hear the other crazed maniacs upstairs trying to get a look at the new guy. He's very submissive to Nala, so I let the others down to meet him one at a time, pretty certain that the introductions will go smoothly since I have a very dog-friendly pack right now.

Now he's so nervous he pees all over the floor, but he quickly decides the dogs are ok, and starts playing like he's one of the gang. I bring him upstairs and let him out into the yard, where he does fine with the cats and even learns the doggie door within 1/2 hour. My kind of dog.

Maybe I'll get lucky tomorrow and a frantic caretaker will show up looking for him . . . He'll then be off in his Porsche to his mansion on the hill, bound for a joyous reunion with his rich mother and father who've decided they must give DDB a million dollar donation for rescuing their baby and keeping him safe from harm overnight.

Ha. One can dream!

Chapter 17

GIVING EVERYTHING UP: BLACK AND WHITE THINKING

ℊ

Look at that cute little face! Baby was an adorable dog, and quickly found a home once we got her off that chain.

Truth: Some people become so overwhelmed by the severe and never-ending need, that they see only two choices: foster way more dogs than they can handle, or stop fostering altogether and leave the rescue world.

Tip: Remember balance, come back to the middle ground. There is another option, once which doesn't involve burnout or the guilt of giving up altogether. You can set limits and foster an amount of dogs that is appropriate for you.

Repeat after me: Giving up is not an option; taking care of both my needs and the needs of the fosters is. I will find the balance.

❦

Burnout is a very real drawback of rescue, and happens as a result of all the things we've talked about up to this point—over-rescuing, problems with and between foster dogs, personal attacks from within the community, no time for yourself, and so on and so forth. Virtually every animal advocacy seminar I've attended features a session on burnout, attempting to guide those rescuers who are in over their heads to a place of greater peace and stability.

The anxiety caused by burnout and overtaxing your psychological and physical well-being can destroy your life. The answer isn't to give up altogether, but to find a path to the balance we all seek.

I'm personally not a fan of prescription meds, although I know many rescuers are on some kind of anti-anxiety medication. I'm not really interested in getting into a Tom Cruise/Brooke Shields brawl with anyone over the pros and cons of prescription medication, and I believe that to each his own.

For myself I choose not to. I have considered taking them in the past, as depression runs on both sides of my family, but I've decided repeatedly to muddle through the rough times without them, and I've grown stronger as a result of toughing it out.

Many people I see on meds, although perhaps less anxious, are also less vital and alive, more prone to letting important tasks slide.

I'm more anxious about what I won't do if I take medication than what I will do without. For myself, I need to feel awake and willing to push through the times when I don't feel like working.

I have tried anxiety medications a time or two with a particularly obsessive or crazy foster dog, like Magnum, but although in the beginning it seemed to quell their fears, over time they built up a tolerance and then had even less of a bite inhibition.

Magnum, chained, 45-lb. dog, 50-lb. chain.

I preferred to deal with the real Magnum. I knew and understand that one better.

Magnum was my foster dog for 2-1/2 years. He was trained to be aggressive on the chain by an immature male caretaker who thought it would be cool to make him mean. When I met

Magnum, he was a 45-pound dog dragging a 50-pound log-ging chain, and he lunged to bite me, ripping my sweatshirt.

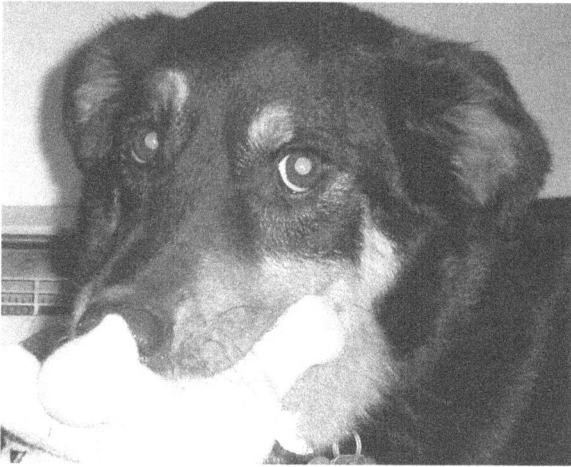

Magnum with one of his stuffed toys.

What this kid really created, rather than a tough, macho dog, was a dog who was so afraid that he thought he'd bite you before you bit him. Although quite a few people thought he should be put down, we persevered, and he lived with me until he became too ill with Pemphigus to go on.

Magnum was wonderful with us; he slept with me, and was usually good with the other dogs, except for the occa-sional food-related argument. It was strangers that brought out his fear aggression. I understood his limitations, and took all steps possible to keep both him and my visitors safe. His anxiety was moderated by a safe, stable environment, and he was contained when necessary for the protection of others. Meds made him groggy, lethargic, but didn't take away the fear aggression. We stopped giving them to him.

However you cope with your anxiety, giving yourself permission to slow down—but not stop—fostering will take a big load off your shoulders. It doesn't have to be all or nothing.

When I slowed down to a manageable amount of foster dogs, I breathed easier, felt better, was happier. The house was cleaner, and I got those little tasks done that tend to slide when I'm overwhelmed.

Try it—get your numbers down—but don't give up. It's not black and white, you CAN be both a foster parent and a happy human.

Foster Diary: I'm thinking about Banshee's scream for help. He's obviously showing signs of separation anxiety, and I wonder how bad it will get.

The vet calls first thing to say that Banshee can go home today—and that he's eating like a horse! Unless his blood-work comes back with something unexpected, we can pick him up this evening.

How cool is that?

Heather arrives with Banshee around 7:00 p.m., having asked if she could be the one to pick him up. I guess I'm not the only one feeling guilty about what happened to him. She goes through medication instructions, and then tells me he needs to remain crated so he doesn't overdo it. We push and shove him into the crate—he won't go willingly—and she and the kids go home.

He is so distressed about being away from me that he's whining, barking, whimpering, and crying. I can't leave him there. It's got to be worse for him to get that stressed, right?

If a bottle of ibuprofen didn't kill him, I highly doubt he's going to keel over now from too much activity.

He's so overjoyed to be with me again that he immediately calms down and lays at my feet, staring at my adoringly, like he just can't believe he's lucky enough to be sharing space with me. Oh, to be so loved!

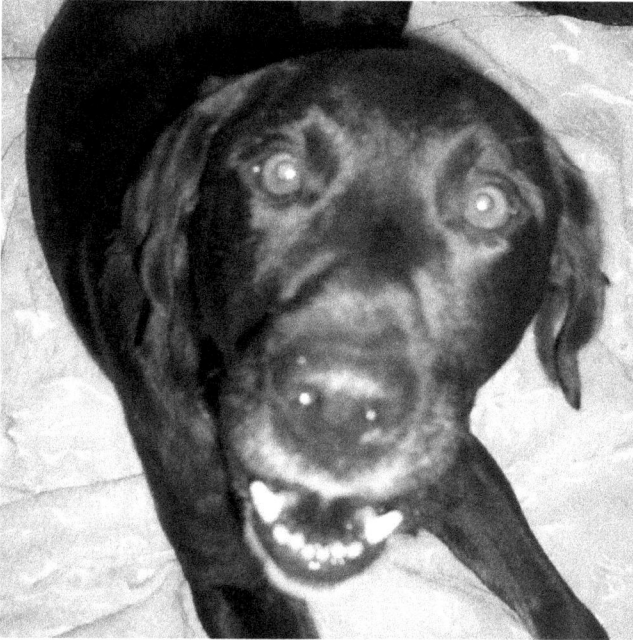

He is so happy to be home that he sleeps quietly and without incident all night in my bedroom with the rest of the dogs. I too am overjoyed, that he made it through, and I kiss and love on him as much as I can to let him know I'm sorry and I missed him.

Chapter 18

FINDING THE MIDDLE GROUND: IT'S ALL A GRAY AREA

⅋

Smokey is one of four blind dogs I fostered in my home. Blind dogs are a delight! They quickly memorize the terrain and get around quite well if given the chance. Smokey came from a West Virginia pen, and I can't imagine living in total isolation and, on top of that, not being able to see what's going on around you. He was adopted into a lovely Washington, D.C. home, and they couldn't have been happier with him as a member of their family. Dogs are treasures, not trash!

Truth: Between black and white, there are many, many shades of gray. Some people can effectively handle one foster dog, while others can handle ten. Remember you don't need to live up to anyone else's expectations, or be the queen of the foster dogs...you just need to work at a pace you can handle and yet still benefits the dogs.

Tip: Understand that there is no magic number of dogs that you should or should not be fostering. The right number is the one you can handle and still find happiness and balance for YOU.

Repeat after me: I'm finding my perfect number of foster dogs, and my perfect balance. I am judging myself by no one else's standards.

※

During my days of heavy foster parenting, the max level of dogs I could handle in my home without getting too crazy was six—but I was much more comfortable, not to mention happier, at four dogs.

I'd promised my kids I'd get down to and keep it at four fosters, which I'd never successfully done for any length of time in the past. I kept it at four for the most part, until I moved from Pennsylvania with DDB and into our own center in Virginia.

The foster homes who get themselves into trouble are the ones who, for whatever reason, overestimate their abilities and think they alone can save the world. They keep taking in the One More and One More and Just this One More even though they haven't gotten homes for the ones that are already laying on their couches. And floors, and beds.

It's a miserable place to be.

If this is you, you'll end up with fighting dogs, frequent vet visits, a torn up house, and a constant mess that weighs you down to the point where you can barely lift your head off the pillow.

You have no time for yourself so that the only 'gift' you give yourself each day is eating too much, abusing prescription medications, smoking, and/or drinking to oblivion.

On the outside you're telling everyone it's all good because you're saving lives. But inside you're a wreck.

Stop right there. Get back on the Balance Train. You've gone overboard, and you need to fix yourself before you go back to fixing broken dogs.

There IS a middle ground, one that we can all find and implement within ourselves.

I remember visiting with one of DDB's area reps in Washington state, Susan, who had been rescuing for well over 10 years. At that time, she was fostering only one dog at a time, because her old dog was just too dog aggressive despite years of training. She couldn't take the stress of fostering so many dogs when his only goal was to destroy them.

In order to keep fostering but keep the dogs safe and her sanity intact, she built a heated area in her garage and a separate fenced area for her foster. She spent time with them as she could each day, and had a dog walker take the foster and her dog out—at separate times—during the day when she wasn't home.

While both she and I would concur that this was not the ideal foster situation, it was a huge step up from where this dog lived—at the end of a chain—and what he or she had before—nothing.

Her foster had a daily walk, love a few times a day, house-training, vetting, a warm bed, and a fenced yard.

Susan found her perfect solution for her circumstances, and when her old dog passed, she reevaluated and created a new fostering situation and a new fostering goal. I commended Susan for finding a way to foster responsibly even under the most difficult of circumstances.

You can do the same. Evaluate your own situation. If you genuinely have a dog that doesn't get along well with others, can you still make something work? Can you keep a dog even on a short-term basis? Often young dogs and puppies get adopted quickly, so your foster situation could have a very quick turn around if you foster young dogs.

I got to the place where I couldn't take in dogs that didn't get along with others. With me traveling so much, we had a real need for harmony in the home; while staff came to care for the dogs and often spent the day there, the dogs didn't have 24/7 company. I knew my limits and chose to stay within them, for the safety of all the dogs and for my own sanity.

Think about what your ideal fostering situation would look like. How can you begin today to work toward that goal?

Foster Diary: I had yet another weekend trip for DDB, and just returned home, which I always dread because I don't know what bad news will be waiting for me this time. The dogs were good while I was gone, in that the neighbors didn't call my staff to complain about the noise, but the dogs have really got the place trashed.

Well, moreso than usual.

Because I have doggie doors, and the area just off the porch ends up mud and dirt instead of grass, the amount of dirt and dust the dogs drag in is unbelievable. I'd literally need to clean for two hours a day, every day, just to stay abreast of it.

Quest, aka The Beast, was a huge but very tolerant akita. This photo was a 'blooper shot,' because we weren't ready when the auto-feature went off, and the leash was in front of Beast's eye. I really like it though because we're laughing and look so happy. It's easy to forget the good times, and these kinds of photos make you realize that although fostering is hard, the joys make it worthwhile.

As it is, my morning ritual consists of getting up, making sure Quest, the Beast, goes out to pee (he would prefer to hold it forever rather than step foot outside—it's an akita thing), and then shutting the dogs downstairs in the office while I clean the upstairs floors.

I check all the dog beds and blankets upstairs, either get clean ones or shake them out, tidy up, and vacuum the floor. I feed the cats on the floor near the doggie door while the dogs are elsewhere—I'm training two semi-ferals to come in so they don't freeze to death—and do the dishes while they are eating.

Most days I also mop the kitchen floor, depending on if we had mud the day before or just dirt. I'm excited about my new steam mop, The Shark, which has given me an almost-white-again kitchen floor. This daily clean-up and feeding takes me about an hour, and doesn't even include the in-depth cleaning that could and should be done. Never enough time in the day!

When I'm away speaking or working for Dogs Deserve Better, my staff often vacuums the floor upstairs before I come home in addition to downstairs duties; I suspect it's to keep me from having a nervous breakdown, which I'm always grateful for.

Dealing with a constantly revolving door of foster dogs reminds me of the movie Groundhog Day, where Bill Murray wakes up every morning to start the same day all over again. I will just get one dog trained and the pack working well to-gether, when I have an adoption or a new dog comes and I have to start all over again. It's exhausting!

Chapter 19

STAND UP FOR YOURSELF: YOU HAVE NEEDS TOO

ဆ

Bandit looked a little mean on the chain, but he was in actuality a total sweetheart. Dogs feel very vulnerable when they are chained. They have a flight or fight instinct, and the chain makes them unable to flee, so they have to prepare to defend themselves. Bandit was unsure if I was there to hurt him or help him, and once freed and made part of an inside home and family, his loving nature made him a wonderful companion.

Truth: You can't give up all your needs for everyone else. If you do, not only will you be miserable, but everyone around you, including your foster dogs, will be miserable too.

Tip: You've got to realize that you DO have needs and these needs are just as important as the needs of your foster dog, your kids, or your husband (or wife). Stand up for yourself.

Repeat after me: I intend to make myself as important as everyone else in my home. No more doormat. That includes husbands (or wives), kids, dogs, and cats. I will meet my needs first and will be then be better able to handle the needs of everyone else.

❧

For many of you, living with a bunch of dogs is your idea of a dream come true. I see it all the time in things my friends post on their Facebook feeds, and I shudder, knowing that I too once thought it would be a little slice of heaven.

If you love animals the way we do, it makes sense that you would want to spend all your time with them. The problem is, when dealing with untrained dogs, the dream can quickly turn into a nightmare, at least until your pack is stable and everyone knows the routine.

This leaves you at an emotional crossroads—if this is my dream come true, why am I now feeling so miserable? There's so much extra work to do that there's just no time for me, everyone else takes up every second of my day.

Dogs are like children, they cannot care for themselves, they make a lot of messes, and they don't help clean up. That is all on you.

When I fostered so many dogs, I gave up anything that

seemed frivolous, which coincidentally were the things that made me feel like ME. I did the same for my kids in many ways, and I don't blame them or anyone else for my mistaken thinking; it was all me, giving up what I loved for my children, the ex, the pets, the organization, my freelance work; all in a showing of classic martyrdom.

I should have been standing up for my rights to alone time, exercise time, reading time, and me time all along, but I didn't.

I used to run, lift weights, date, play, all the kind of things that normal, self-centered people get to do. And some of it I even did well, except for the marrying part.

That was all BC—Before Children, BDDB—Before Dogs Deserve Better, and BFD—Before Foster Dogs.

Then I spent 20 years giving and giving and giving and giving to everyone but myself...I gave myself nothing except for too much food (and sometimes booze) and too much guilt because it was never enough.

I couldn't make them happy.

But I wasn't happy either, and my unhappiness spilled over into my family.

Is this you too? Are you happy? Honestly?

If you're insisting you're overjoyed, but meanwhile you're 50 pounds overweight, taking pills to calm your nerves, smoking, and/or drinking every night before falling into bed to repeat the whole process the next day, I don't call that happy, I call that denial.

And you just may have a bad case of it.

You probably have little energy zappers of your own at home, your foster dogs, of course, but also a husband, children, other needy family members, not to mention your 'real' work and your rescue group. Oi! Who wouldn't be miserable?

It's time to take a good look at yourself in whatever mirror is closest. I know it's hard. Take a good look, and tell yourself this one thing: "I love you. I'm sorry. I'll start to figure out what you need right now, today. I promise."

It's time. Think of yourself. You're not going to abandon everyone else, but you must make yourself important too. I give you not only my permission to start taking time for YOU, but also my blessing.

Foster Diary: I've been home from my DDB trip since Monday, but it's taken me a couple days to start feeling like myself again.

I've learned that I can't let myself wallow in fear and sadness, it's a sinking ship that just pulls me under. Lynn Grabhorn says you've got to 'open your valve,' in order to start creating change in your life, which really means open your heart and start experiencing positive feelings. Allow good things in, instead of shutting off and shutting down, which only brings in more of the bad.

I'm finally getting to that today, and doing my community service at the library has been my path to opening my valve.

If you're thinking I'm so altruistic that the mere thought of serving my community by dusting library shelves and moving books opens my heart, you couldn't be more wrong.

What it does mean is that the four hours I'm slaving away at the library for the egregious crime of saving a dog from death, I'm listening to my iPod. And on my iPod I have, mixed in with the songs in shuffle mode, Grabhorn's book *Excuse Me, Your Life is Waiting*, broken down into 45 chapters. Ah, nothing like a little self-help to brighten your day!

So instead of feeling angry and considering this a time suck like I used to, I've turned it into a chance to boost my soul and open my heart valve so that my life can take a turn for the better. By the time I leave the library, I feel more open and ready to take on the world again.

Upon arriving home four hours later, I hear a local woman on the answering machine asking for help for the neighbor's beagle. I sigh, knowing it's freezing out, and call her back. Turns out the poor little thing is in Grazierville, just four miles from me, living outside in a crate.

The neighbors are willing to give her up.

She is crying, saying she "already has a dog, so she can't take her"—here we go again, ONE dog?—but seeing her out there freezing is killing her. (Not killing her enough to take her in, apparently...)

There goes my positive feelings! Argh. That was fast.

She tells me the neighbors said I could go by and take the dog even if they aren't there, and I laugh and say "Yeah, right!" I don't think so.

I'm not taking ANY dog (that isn't dying at least) without a signed action form releasing ownership of the dog to Dogs Deserve Better; what happened with Kanook and Doogie emphasizes the position.

She later calls back to tell me the girl will be home the next morning.

Sigh. I'll be there.

Chapter 20

STOP BEATING YOURSELF UP: GUILT GETS YOU NOWHERE FAST

❧

Former foster dog Spot enjoying a kong. Most doggie parents and foster parents take advantage of kongs and other tricks of the trade to keep dogs' minds engaged. These toys (there are many elaborate ones on the market, check them out) help the dogs by providing mental stimulation and enjoyment, and help us as foster parents by cutting out some of the behaviors that makes our lives more difficult! Win/win!

Truth: Most of us, whereupon screwing up, feel guilty and wallow around in that guilt for days, weeks, months. We can't move forward while stuck in guilt.

Tip: Give it up! You must let go of feeling bad about yourself for a faulty decision you may have made. As long as your intentions were pure, and you've learned as a result of this action, you've got to let it go in order to continue your mission.

Repeat after me: I harbor only good intentions for my foster dogs. Even though I sometimes make mistakes, I know I never intended to cause harm; I learn from my actions, and continue moving forward in a positive direction.

෧෮

We all screw up. I could spend the rest of this book listing my missteps with foster dogs, some of which have had serious consequences. And some of them, like Banshee and the ibuprofen, have been extremely hard to let go of my guilt over.

In fact, if Banshee hadn't survived, I'm pretty sure I'd still be hanging onto that guilt despite my best advice to you, my advice to both of us right here on this page. But I know it would not be healthy, and it wouldn't help me love myself or my other foster dogs. It wouldn't bring Banshee back.

Without the ability to love ourselves, we cannot truly give love to others, no matter whether they be dogs or people. And we can't love ourselves or anyone else when we're dragging around a boatload of guilt and shame.

I know that Banshee's angel-self, if he HAD lost his life, would have forgiven me, knowing I never meant to cause him harm. He would have taken those couple months and all the love and joy he received over never having been given a chance at a real life. Over still living stuck out on that chain.

I'm considerably lucky to have him; I know it, I value it, and I love him all the more for almost losing him.

I'm sure if you've done any amount of fostering, something bad has happened to one of your fosters that you too could be guilt-ridden over. People who don't foster are quick to jump to conclusions and judge others as not being good enough— but we must remember that dogs are living beings, and have wills and minds of their own!

They do things; and whether you believe it or not, often they do bad things and things you don't expect and things you were not prepared for, and things that will get them or someone else hurt or killed.

If you don't believe me, grab yourself a couple of foster dogs and get back with me again in a few weeks.

One of my good friends, Gordon, is an older gentleman and a big supporter of our cause. He has stood side by side with me chained to doghouses in support of the dogs, and is very passionate and vocal on their behalf. Yet Gordon doesn't foster, has never fostered, and has only one little doggie at home who is the love of his life.

Gordon's view of dogs is sheltered, and he believes in the fairy tale world where all dogs are good all the time. But dogs are living, breathing creatures, and their behavior can be very much like children; sometimes good, sometimes bad, and sometimes very, very bad, screaming like banshees if you will.

Gordon doesn't understand that there can be negative consequences to dealing with dogs en masse, and frequently argues with me when I try to explain to him what dogs are capable of.

He's flat out told me he doesn't believe it, and I realize that despite all that's been written to show both the good and the bad that come with living with dogs, most of America also believes a very naive fairy tale.

I admit that I, too, was totally naive about dogs before I started Dogs Deserve Better, and I never would have believed it before I started living it.

When I told him that dogs fight—even those you think won't—and it happens fast, and you have to do whatever you can do to get that fight stopped before someone is dead, he couldn't fathom it.

It's happened in my home, and it's awful for everyone involved, but the most memorably horrifying dog fight I've witnessed was when I was volunteering after Katrina. My best friend Tracy and I were working the feeding stations during the day, which meant we weren't really getting to interact with animals at all outside of some feral cats. So we started going over to a rescue who'd set up there after our shift to walk a few dogs for a hands-on doggie fix.

There was a pit bull there, God love him, covered in scars and who, I would assume, had been used in dogfighting. He was a very nice dog—with people—but I personally would never have taken the chance on putting him in with other dogs. Common sense would say a big NO to that.

There was a rescuer there who hated that this dog wasn't allowed to go into the 'dog park' with the other dogs. You can see where this story is heading and it ain't pretty...

The dog park was actually a swimming pool at the school that was the rescue's temporary home, full of murky, slimy and bug-infested water; it was the only location at this make-shift facility that had a fence. The dogs who got along well with other dogs were allowed to run around and play in the swimming pool area for an hour or so each day, and were watched over by one or two volunteers.

Being naive, and by no means intending to do harm, the rescuer took it upon himself to put the pit bull into the dog park with the ten or so other dogs. This pit, only doing what he'd been trained to do, promptly grabbed an old, long-haired shepherd by the throat, and proceeded to do his best to take him out fast and hard.

The shepherd's screaming was so disturbing I can find no words to describe it. We weren't right there at the time, but we ran for the dog park with everyone else to see if we could help, although I was sure someone—a dog—was dying.

All the major players and volunteers with the rescue who were authorized to do so ran into the dog park to get the pit off the shepherd, while the rest of us stood outside the fence watching in horror and disbelief.

They did everything you can imagine to get that dog off the other dog. Kicking, pulling, prying, lifting his legs, pouring water over his head...everything. And I must have blocked it out, because I can't remember what finally got the pit off the shepherd...but they either pushed both dogs in the pool of murky water, or they used a large metal pipe to pry open the pit's jaws.

After what seemed like forever but was probably only a few minutes, the shepherd was finally free. I believed he would die regardless after hearing his tortured shrieks, but turns out that his long hair was a blessing. Although most of the hair on his neck was gone, we were told that he was going to live, and I hoped that was the case. His survival was a testament to quick action and a sincere desire to save a life on the part of many people.

Tracy and I were so distraught from witnessing the event that we had to drive immediately to Denny's for a piece of chocolate pie. We were actually shaking as we sat in the restaurant, and it took us about an hour to calm down enough to go back to the Fema tent where we were staying.

This horrific story exemplifies how quickly a bad decision by a good person can cost a life in the space of five minutes. Yes, one guy bought into the story that all dogs are warm and fuzzy all the time, but that doesn't make him a bad person; he learned a big lesson that day.

I assume he believed that pit bulls have been falsely maligned, and he's right to an extent; but when someone trains any dog of any breed to be a dangerous weapon, expecting that training to easily drop away overnight is extremely naive.

This rescuer was beside himself with guilt and remorse. I saw his face when we were leaving, and he was holding his head in his hands, his eyes reflecting a soul in the depths of Hell. I hope he was able to forgive himself and go back to helping the dogs. A little wiser, granted, but still full of hope in his ability to make a difference.

Whatever mistakes you've made, they were probably made from a place of innocence. Be open to doing it better, learning from your mistakes, but stop judging yourself and stop accepting the misjudgments of others. You can continue to make a difference, learning as you go. That's the best you can do as a human being, and the most others can reasonably expect of you.

Foster Diary: I'm done with the morning feeding and cleaning routine, and as soon as my two staff members get in to work I tell them I'm leaving to pick up the beagle. We're happy it's a girl at least—there are far too many boys here, and the thought of housetraining another male right now makes us all want to scream.

In case you're new to fostering, housetraining rescued males is typically much harder than housetraining females. Why? Because males that come from bad situations, i.e. living outside, are not neutered and as such are in possession of a high sex drive and are ambitious enough to pee on every single thing in your house as a means of marking their territory. Yeah, gross!

They have no idea the behavior is not wanted or valued by you (that you really don't enjoy your house smelling like eau de dog), therefore the smartest thing to do is to leash them to you for two days so you can watch them every second while you correct the behavior and take them outside to pee instead. Repeatedly.

As you can imagine, this is both time-consuming and annoying, but it's a skill that has to be mastered and mastered quickly by the dog so that he has the tools necessary to find a forever home, and—equally importantly—you can retain your sanity.

Females, on the other hand, just pee because they have to

go, so if you miss their signal and don't get them outside in time you just end up with a puddle on the floor. Much easier to catch and clean up!

I arrive at the trailer, and the young guy is sitting in the car, listening to music while he waits for me. He gets out, introduces himself, and walks me over to meet the dog. We are joined by his girlfriend, and I actually like the kids, a rare occurrence.

Despite the fact that the dog is living in a crate, they have made every effort to keep her as warm as possible. She has a sleeping bag covering the crate, and straw stuffed all throughout the crate. There is fresh food and water, and she's not gobbling it down, so she's obviously well-fed.

The dog, who we later name Puddles, is a bit iffy with me, snapping a time or two, but I don't take it too seriously...after all, she's a little beagle, how bad can it be! I'm sure we'll work it out.

The story goes that the boy's father dumped the dog on them; she'd belonged to his uncle where she was not only chained, but abused and starved too. These kids didn't want a dog, and didn't know what to do with her. They knew it was wrong to keep her outside, and they wanted her to have a real home, which they weren't prepared or willing to give her. At least they were honest, which I always appreciate.

They sign the release papers with a sigh of relief, and I don't think they'll be giving her too much though in the future.

When I get Puddles home, Kim takes one look at her and decides she'd like to foster her. Woohoo for me! Since her dog Zoe died, she only has one dog, another older beagle named Hannah that we got from a similar situation. Puddles is so cute, though, and Kim can't wait to see how she and Hannah look together.

I take Puddles to her house after work, and stand outside with Puddles on a leash while Kim goes to get Hannah for the introductions. We plan to give them a good walk before they go inside, to wear them out and create some camaraderie between them on neutral territory so they're more likely to accept each other. Hannah remains standoffish, but she eventually warms up to Puddles throughout the course of the evening.

I love it when a plan comes together. That's one dog off my plate!

Chapter 21

MAKE A PLAN:
TAKE CARE OF YOU TOO

ઝ

Dallas was a very sweet yet unsocialized boy due to spending his life on the chain. It takes a lot of time and patience to bring shy dogs around, but he found a wonderful and loving home that kept in touch with me and are still my friends through social media today.

Truth: Just saying you are going to take better care of yourself is rarely enough to make it happen. Most of us in rescue take care of everyone but ourselves...and then live or die to pay the price.

Tip: You've got to make a plan for taking care of you. In fact,

I challenge you to commit to 1/2 hour a day from here on out to do something you love but no longer do, because you just don't have time. Make time.

Repeat after me: Today I start taking care of me, too, because I matter. Today I commit to 1/2 hour of [fill in the blank]. That's just the beginning of my new, shiny plan for making ME count!

Face it, if you don't take care of yourself, no one else is going to. We all rush around taking care of everyone else so we don't have to face our own issues, our own crap. If we're busy giving dogs what they need, or kids what they need, or partners what they need, there's no time left over to give ourselves what we need.

And that's usually just the way we want it. There's nothing scarier than facing our own inadequacies, needs, dreams...or failures.

Facing the fact that you eat too much, drink too much, take too many drugs, or smoke too much as a negative path to giving yourself something—anything—is the last thing we are comfortable dealing with.

When we take a good look at these issues, we immediately feel scared, ashamed, overwhelmed, hopeless, and helpless to make a change. The motivation isn't there to make ourselves happy.

We don't feel worthy; we don't deserve happiness. People will say we're self-centered or selfish. We can't live with that...

then they won't like us.

Why do the majority of us feel so unworthy of life's abundance? We are ALL worthy!

I personally grew up in an abusive home, and watched my father try to kill my mother at the age of 16. To say I never felt worthy would be an understatement. Me and my two brothers were nothing to my father except emotional punching bags, and my mother was closed down and protecting herself. There was no one to protect the children.

Given time and distance, I can see that in all likelihood no matter what kind of childhood I experienced, I'd have found a way to feel unworthy because of it. My kids probably will too, even though I've tried hard to be a more forgiving and loving parent, to do better than was done to me.

Isn't it just easier to doom ourselves to failure before we even start? To have a good excuse for not even trying?

My favorite Ellen DeGeneres joke of all time went thus, to the best of my recollection: "After 10 years in therapy I realized I thought I was 'A piece of crap that the world revolves around.' " I still chuckle over it, because I can thoroughly relate. Is this the truth for you too?

My family was supposedly good Christian folk, which really meant we swept all the abuse and fear under the rug, pretending everything was A-OK when it wasn't.

I spent many years trying to be a good person despite the horrific way I felt inside, trying to make up for whatever I must have done to deserve the mistreatment, trying to get love from both my parents, still trying to win love from my father after all the abuse.

I was so deep in my denial, I didn't even realize my childhood was abusive until I was 30. Suddenly something clicked, and I wanted to figure out how I got into this crappy position. I wanted to feel better about myself. I started to devour self-help books, trying anything to somehow feel better. Most of it worked in the short term, but it's a full-time job trying to evolve and grow into something worthy.

Or, more accurately, to learn to accept that I am worthy just as I am. There's the challenge.

I'd like you to ponder not only how you got into this boat but how you're going to get yourself out of it; no more time for wallowing. No matter what, promise me that today you will take 30 minutes for YOU.

Foster Diary: We're now seeing some major issues with Banshee related to separation anxiety. When there is someone home with him, he is, while not a perfect angel, certainly not ripping anything up or destroying anything.

But it's becoming more and more apparent that he must be contained when no one is here for his own safety.

I've been coming home to, or staff's been finding when arriving at work, complete mayhem and destruction. He chewed up a bunch of DDB's Holiday auction items, reaching up on top of the table and pulling down a box full of goodies, and demolished the entire contents. He has destroyed papers, boxes, books, you name it. Whatever he can get ahold of and fits into his mouth.

When I'm home, he hangs out with me every second, plays with his ball, undertakes normal energetic dog behavior, but isn't destructive. As soon as I walk out that door, though, all holy Hell is breaking loose!

Today I have to go into town, and Kim isn't here, so he'll be spending quality time in the crate. I normally use the crates as little as possible, because I'm a big fan of freedom. I know they have their place and their uses, but I just hate to confine a dog more than is absolutely necessary, especially after what they've lived through on a chain or in a pen.

However, I can no longer deny that with Banshee it has become an absolute necessity. Not only is he destroying my house and my sanity, but he will end up destroying himself by getting ahold of something else poisonous, and he won't be so lucky this time.

I attempt to explain the whole sordid mess to him as I toss his ball into the crate, thereby luring him in too. Luckily, he'll go just about anywhere for a ball. He's not really buying my explanations though, looking at me quizzically once he's trapped and wondering why he's being tortured so.

I remind him it's his own fault; it's this or certain death by his own jaws sooner or later, so he might as well get used to it. He'll be spending a fair amount of time in here from now on, since I can't stay here 24/7!

With me traveling so much, crating a dog for an extended period of time is not feasible. There can be days the dogs will be alone from 8:00 p.m. after Kim comes down to check on them and give them a snack, until the next morning when she comes back in to take care of everyone. That's why we have the two fenced areas and the two doggy doors, so that the pack can be separated into safe numbers; they can go out to the bathroom as needed, and then come in and sleep in the warmth of the home.

Having to crate Banshee will indeed create a real logistical nightmare for us.

When I get back from my errands, I discover yet another challenge to crating Banshee...he can't hold his bladder, and the crate is sopping wet with pee. I've noticed that he pees often, and copious amounts, but I thought that he was just doing that because he was so hyper. But now he has peed all through the crate after only a few hours alone.

This just isn't going to work.

We're going to have to find another way to keep him safe and contained, with access to the outside, because none of us can go on in this fashion.

Chapter 22

WHAT DO YOU LIKE? IT MATTERS

ဆ

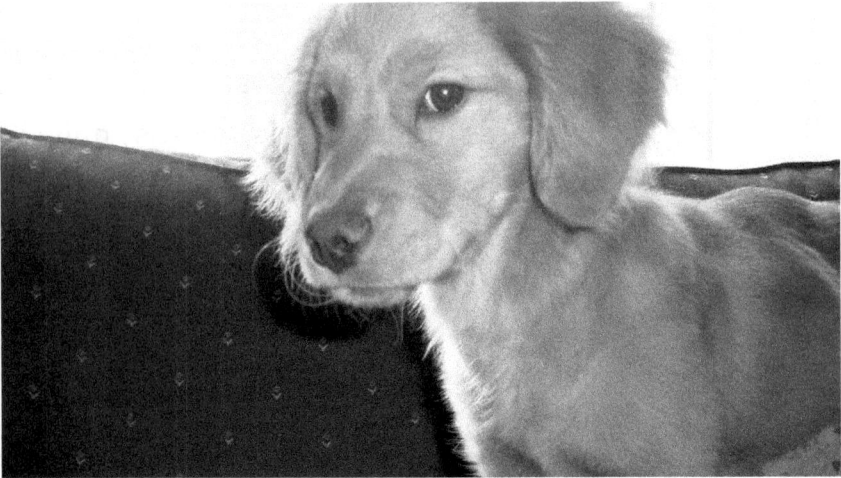

Look at that adorable little puppy face! Sabrina was a golden retriever puppy I fostered, and she loved, loved, loved to play with the bigger dogs, following them everywhere. Puppies remind you of the joys of life, the importance of living in the moment, and rediscovering your own light.

Truth: There are things you like, you know there are, that you never let yourself do because you are overwhelmed with foster dogs and daily life. What are those things?

Tip: Now is the time to figure out what you enjoy, really enjoy, to do. Remember. Besides taking care of dogs. Things that just make you happy. Just because.

Repeat after me: Today I will make a list of all the things I like to do, or liked to do, BD—before dogs. Then I will pick one and do it.

∝℧

It really does matter what you enjoy doing. It doesn't matter to me—I just want you to be happy—but it matters to you. I know you like being a doggie foster mom. Maybe you even love it. But you've let yourself get overwhelmed with that job for too long, and it's time to ease back and make joy a priority.

Taking care of others, even when you love them dearly, takes a lot out of you. And even though you may feel it's truly a labor of love, there's still that small, quiet voice in your silent soul whispering, "What about me?"

You've ignored it, like most women in rescue, giving yourself a little extra chocolate or rich food treats every day in an effort to feed your soul. It hasn't worked. All this has done is given you, me, all of us, a collective big fat butt and by extension more sadness. I know, I've lived that dream.

I look at photos of myself when I first started DDB, and I was thinnish and looked downright hot on occasion. And happy! Then over time, rescue after rescue, excuse after excuse for not exercising or spending quality time with myself, I put on a pound or two here, a pound or three there, until by the time I left DDB I didn't even know who it was looking out of that photo! Scary!

But those days are behind us now. Time to feed our soul

with something besides chocolate and pasta.

So tell me, what is it you like?

There is one gift I gave myself during the writing of *Scream Like Banshee* and carried it through until today, so I'll go first, and I'm excited to tell you...I've started reading fiction again! This was one of my great loves as an introverted child who spent a lot of time alone on the farm; I had the best vocabulary in the school from devouring piles of books from the library, and, lest I forget, my mother's Harlequin romances!

When I grew up and got serious about changing my life and making a difference, I stopped 'allowing' myself to read fiction. I always read self-help books—because by gum I needed them—but allowed myself nothing that was frivolous and would make me feel like I was frittering away my time and my life.

I had no immediate intentions of taking up fiction reading again, because I still had goals I viewed as very important to accomplish in life. But talking to you about the concept of doing more to bring yourself joy, and remembering what I liked as a child, got me thinking that maybe, just maybe, I could let a little fiction light back into my life.

And I still love it! Maybe a little too much, actually...because I could spend the rest of my life just reading and putting myself into the characters of the book. Ah, now I remember why I cut myself off before! But, I remind myself that balance is the key...so I set time limits in the morning and at night before sleep for reading. It's working.

So tell me...what can you do for an hour tonight that will bring you joy? Put the dogs to bed an hour early, and then go for it! You know where I'll be...

Foster Diary: I call the humane officer again and leave yet another message about Kanook. I still have seen no signs of him, and apparently O.G. thinks I should just be moving along now. Nothing more to see here.

He doesn't like the little woman all up in his business. I am by nature a shy person, and so the thought of putting myself in people's faces time and time again is very disturbing to me and goes against my nature.

I know that people think I'm so big and brave because of what I do for chained dogs and what I did for Doogie, but even though I have a very real sense of right and wrong, and by that I mean moral right and wrong, in other ways I'm just as much a coward as the next girl. I know, I hate it too!

To his credit, O.G. does call me back this time, and tells me that he hasn't seen Kanook either, but he knows that she took him to a vet in Altoona; he saw the records. He promises to get a look at him asap.

I know you're probably as frustrated reading this as I am having to write it. I'm well aware it sucks. Although we may lose many battles, especially in these initial stages of the war, we will not lose the war; we have right on our side. Remember that.

It sucks that Kanook has been relegated to the status of a lost battle. I know he's a living, breathing creature, one that I was privileged to know, love, and then lose.

I'm sorry, Baby.

Chapter 23

CHILDHOOD MEMORIES: THE CLUES YOU WILL FIND THERE

&

One of my first staff members with Dogs Deserve Better, Bronwyn, working from my Pennsylvania home. You'd have thought we were a cat rescue instead of a dog rescue! I see seven cats.

Truth: Sometimes you've become so lost in the daily shoulds and musts, and in taking care of everyone but you, that you truly, truly can't even remember what it is that would give you some joy.

Tip: If you still haven't a clue what brings you a little slice of happiness pie, search through your childhood memories or photo albums. There you will find your clues.

Repeat after me: When I was a child I loved [blank], and [blank], and [blank]. I'd like to try those three activities again, starting today!

◌

What is that saying; when I became a (wo)man I put away childish things? While we may have followed that advice and put away our childhood loves, I say it's in our best interest to dig them back up and give them another look-see.

What would you uncover?

What was your greatest passion as a child? Do you remember?

A recent craze I've been seeing online is coloring for adults, and the friends I've seen taking this up are reporting that they find it very soothing and it brings them peace. I'm thinking of giving it a whirl myself. I'm sure it brings back memories of a more carefree youth.

My four favorite activities as a young person were spending time with the animals, reading novels, learning other languages, and drawing.

When I first entered college at Penn State University, my soul begged me to become an Art Major, but my head told me that was frivolous; I listened to my head and became a Business Major.

Then I filled my schedule with art and language classes.

We can trick our soul, stuff down our desires, but they will either find their way out on their own or slowly kill us. Embrace your loves!

After a year and a half in college—and wanting to be like my older brother—I jaunted off to the Air Force, but even here my soul found a way. I discovered they had a linguistic career option so I took the DLAB, the language exam for the armed services, to see if I could qualify to become one myself. I scored a 152, which was the highest they'd ever seen at the Pittsburgh enlistment station, and I went on to serve almost five years as a Czech linguist.

While I was in the service I continued taking college courses, mostly language and art, finally embraced my inner artist, and ended up graduating with a B.A. in Art from the University of Maryland.

The soul finds its way. Listen to it!

When I yearned to discover a higher purpose, a mission for my life, I was confounded. I was an artist, but as a graphic designer I was doing art to please everyone else, and I didn't feel I was changing the world. I wasn't happy in my career. I had been a linguist, but the time for that vocation seemed to be over.

What next? What would give me fulfillment?

When I moved back to Pennsylvania with my young son Rayne, I was very troubled by seeing chained dogs. Since I had grown up with a chained dog, it ate away at me, and I couldn't believe it was 20 years later and Americans were still chaining their dogs.

But what could I do about it? I was just one person. It was

too hard.

People told me "You can't do anything, no one cares."

They said "I agree with you, but it's really not our business how they take care of their dogs."

They said "Just because we wouldn't treat ours like that, doesn't mean we can tell them what to do."

I didn't want people to not like me. I didn't want to die standing up for the rights of chained dogs. So I stuffed the dream down. I was scared.

When I began to search in earnest for my mission, I came across one of the best books on excavating your childhood loves and developing your soul's path that I have ever found— *You Already Know What to Do*, by Sharon Franquemont. I made myself do EVERY exercise (this is crucial, don't skip the exercises!) and the knowledge I gained crystallized my vision and dreams.

I WOULD stand up for chained dogs, whether that stand be solitary or others came to stand with me. I would face the death that might come as a result of squaring off against animal abusers. I knew in my gut that anyone who could chain a dog was probably not the nicest person.

I determined to do it anyway.

So there I was again, embroiled in and now working for my third childhood passion—animals.

I spent the next thirteen years working feverishly for chained dogs, which included spending 828 hours chained to a doghouse, something not too many folks are willing to do.

What were your childhood loves? So far I've embraced and explored all of mine—reading, drawing, languages, and animals—and I think I may now try my hand at fiction writing, since I love reading so much. I could create a Shero who takes down dog chainers in her spare time. Yeah!

I highly recommend Sharon's book if you don't know or remember what your childhood loves were, or even if you do... you may learn a lot more about yourself, discovering hidden gems and desires, than you ever realized.

Foster Diary: In the middle of the night it hits me...the solution to my Banshee problem.

I just need to combine the crate WITH the doggie door! So that when he comes running in from the outside, he's automatically in the crate, thereby protecting both himself and our property! But, he can run outside again whenever he needs to go pee!

Boom! I know...it's not rocket science, but it might as well be to me. When that solution hits me as I lay awake and pondering, you'd have thought I'd died and gone to heaven. Bliss.

We have a super size crate, and all we have to do is somehow rig it up in front of the doggie door downstairs, manage to keep it there in a way that he can't push the crate and squeeze out, and we're golden.

Thank Dog! I finally see light at the end of the tunnel for me and my silly-boy Banshee; I love him even more now that I know there's an end in sight to my dilemma.

Chapter 24

SAVORING THE JOY: YOUR NEW FREE TIME

℘

Founder was a very old shepherd I fostered who still had many playful bones in her body. She embraced the joy of rediscovering her youth, and you can too! Take your pump out of the dog's mouth, dress like you mean it, and head out on the town. Do something for you!

Truth: When you start to achieve that balance between fostering dogs and taking care of yourself, you'll discover that you have time for you, you really do, and it brings a quiet joy to know you matter.

Tip: Let yourself delight in finding the balance. The true ecstasy of allowing yourself some fun, some you time, some frivolity.

Repeat after me: I am not only finding the joy in my life again, but I am choosing to revel in that joy. I am FREE!

❧

Let's not sugar-coat it: animal rescuers know the worst of humanity. We truly do. It is so easy to spend all your time in hatred, pain and negativity, but if you do that, they win. They win because they've taken your soul and destroyed you. Please don't allow that to happen! You deserve better.

You must make room in your life for love, laughter, and activities that bring you joy.

I believe that the energy we put out of our bodies and souls each day attracts like energy. When we allow ourselves and our psyches to be engulfed by the atrocities we know are going on in the world, it brings down every aspect of our lives.

For me the question and the struggle always remains the same: how do we address and confront the abuse we see in the world without becoming victims of the negative energy put out by the perpetrators of the abuse? I still don't have an easy answer, but I believe we somehow must keep trying to better the world without losing ourselves in the process.

To illustrate how negative energy attracts like energy, let's look at my life at the time of the Doogie trial. I had been putting out negative energy for quite awhile, totally engrossed in the rescue movement and reading horror story after horror story about what people do to dogs and animals in general.

Then Doogie came along, and now I was the one personally faced with the evils perpetrated by man. I chose to stand against the evil, but became totally embroiled in what negative energy does when you thwart it. My energy spiralled to it's second lowest point ever (unbelievably, there was a lower point to come), swallowing my soul in a mire of negativity, fear, hatred, and anger.

Even though I knew I took the right action on behalf of the dog, I felt victimized by those in power. At one point the District Attorney told the local news that I was "worse than the worst hardened criminal." Because I rescued a dying dog, I was somehow worse than a serial killer? In what universe?

My output of negative energy drew in other negative events, one after the other. In addition to the Doogie trial, my ex went after me in court for my daughter using my 'crime' as leverage to take her, and I was no longer strong enough emotionally to understand the situation or to fight. I was so depressed I told my attorney I couldn't go back to court again, so the judge gave her to my ex. I screwed up.

Then, I was attacked by one of my foster dogs, sending me to the hospital in an ambulance.

I was lucky to even pick my head up off the pillow each morning and begin another day. I would hear my daughter's bus drive by my house and just lay there and sob. The only thing I could possibly do to survive was to put one foot in front of the other each day until I was capable of handling more.

I finally realized I couldn't stay in that emotional place any longer or it would kill me. I began to take action to change my life, and so can you. If we don't, the negativity will bury us alive, and good people deserve better than that.

During my years with DDB, we had many problems with folks who signed on as representatives for us then proved themselves to be untrustworthy. In just one example, we fired an area rep for overloading herself to the point where she robbed Peter to pay Paul, she lied, she took in way too many dogs, and she ended up with a big mess on her hands.

By extension so did Dogs Deserve Better.

I can't say the girl didn't start with good intentions, maybe she did. But when your need to help becomes a sickness in itself and you lie to cover up the mess you've created, it's time to get some psychological help, not for the dogs but for yourself. None of us are super-human.

When confronted with the mounting evidence of a major problem, the rep denied all allegations, blamed everyone but herself, and had people e-mailing saying we were awful for firing one of the best rescuers in the world.

Meanwhile, we were making good faith payments to vets we didn't even know existed, adopters who were sending in complaints, and all-in-all cleaning up a disaster not of our making.

This was a person seriously, seriously in over her head. She was not able to pay these dogs' vet bills, most of which were not formerly chained dogs, but she was making promises to pay and then avoiding the vets. She was having big-time dog fights when these dogs were able to get at each other, as confirmed by vet bills we received, and one dog even had to have his leg amputated as a result.

I know accidents happen when you foster dogs. But the more dogs you take in, the greater your chances of becoming severely overwhelmed becomes; very ugly occurrences WILL happen as a result.

You don't want or need that. By all means, don't avoid all dire stories, but don't embroil yourself. Create limits that enable you to help yet keep your sanity. You are no good to the dogs if you kill yourself trying to do too much.

But I digress.

You're finding your joy now, so this isn't you anymore, right? You are wiser, know how to say no, and know when to say no. You are not overwhelming yourself, and you are able to enjoy the fosters you have, while relishing the newfound free time you've garnered for yourself. Just you, and no one else.

Let Loose!

Live it UP!

Love Yourself!

Love Your Activities, Your Significant Other, Your Kids, Your Dogs, Your Work!

The book that changed my life during that year of suffering was called *Excuse Me, Your Life is Waiting*, by Lynn Grabhorn, which I previously mentioned listening to while doing community service at the library. Of all the self-help books I've read in the last 15 years, and there have been many, this book led me to the biggest personal change. I read and listened to it over and over again.

Through it I learned how to take control of my emotions and negative feelings and turn them around to positive feelings so that I no longer wallowed in stress, shame, anger, or fear. I learned techniques I still use today when I realized I'm wallowing in negative emotions.

I had to work at it, really work, but I made tremendous emotional progress because of it. I downloaded it into the hard drive disk of the DDB van, so that when I traveled for the organization I could listen to it for reinforcement of the messages and receive a reminder and an instant lift.

If you buy and read one book as a result of my recommendations, make it *Excuse Me, Your Life is Waiting*. If you become a student of this book, I promise you WILL change your life.

Foster Diary: It works! Yesterday I rigged up the Banshee containment system, BCS, and today came home from the store to a safe dog, a pee-free crate, and an intact house.

Wow.

You'd think I just won a Nobel Prize, I'm that damn thrilled.

This proves that I have to be continually evolving in order to address the needs of my foster dogs, and the old tried and true methods don't always work.

It also proves there's always a way. Sometimes you just have to think outside the dog box.

I've found my way this time, and hopefully Banshee will have a long and love-filled life before him because of it. And I will savor my remaining sanity that revels in the good parts of Banshee and easily deals with the crazier parts.

Sometimes, that's enough to make for the perfect day.

Chapter 25

LOOKING GOOD AGAIN: YOU DESERVE TO FEEL GOOD ABOUT YOURSELF!

❧

Flaunt it like you mean it! Todd was one of my many foster kitties over the years, and he earned the nickname Hot Toddy because he was downright sexy and he knew it. Connect with your inner Hot Toddy today!

Truth: You feel better when you look better, and you look better when you feel better. Our bodies, minds, and souls are connected. Our looks tend to be the first thing we let slide when taking on too many foster dogs, and it's time to start tending to our bodies as well as our souls.

Tip: Think about what goes into your mouth. Fill your fridge with fruits and veggies, (and a little dark chocolate, duh), but no donuts, or whatever your Achilles heel happens to be. If it's not there, you can't eat it.

Repeat after me: I'm a hot, sexy babe (or dude), and I deserve to look and feel good! My looks are as sweet as my soul!

I don't want to harp about our weight. I know we're kind, wonderful rescue folks with hearts of gold, who don't deserve to be told we're fat. But let's face it, some of us just lean that direction; I count myself among those who do.

I wish it were something I could truthfully say I've conquered by now, but it's always been an ongoing battle for me, and it got worse once I started fostering dogs. I am eating a carrot as I type, if that means anything? A nice, big, juicy, organic carrot?

I'm kinda like Oprah...I conquer my weight, or at least wrestle it into submission, and then when I take my focus off the situation it gets away from me and I'll suddenly realize I've hit 180 or higher. That's usually when I'm feeling totally overwhelmed with life and commitments (including foster dogs), and I make no time to focus on me or time to care about how I look.

At those times I hate the message I send to the world

about myself.

You may hate your message too.

So what do we do about it? Take action!

What would that look like for you? What actions can you commit to today to make your health and appearance better in the near future? Please give this some serious thought, and make a plan to implement changes in your life. You deserve to feel good about yourself.

Last year when I left Dogs Deserve Better, I was at my lowest point ever, for reasons which I'll reveal to you soon. I looked in the mirror, and saw a woman who weighed 187 pounds, was firmly ensconced in middle age, and who didn't feel good about herself. Not only that, but I feared my health was taking a turn for the worse.

Heart and blood clot issues—as well as high cholesterol— run on both sides of my family of origin. I was becoming concerned about my heart status, as I got winded just walking up a flight of steps, and sometimes I felt like there was a heavy band tightening across my chest.

I decided enough was enough. I downloaded the Lose It app on my phone, and started counting calories every single day. I also exercised daily, starting with walking, and gradually moved up to running and the elliptical. I've only missed 20 days of exercise in the past year, and I normally do yoga, 45 minutes on the elliptical, and then a short round of weights for some muscle, for a total of an hour a day.

I've lost 31 pounds, and have a maintainable goal in mind of 150, so I have 6 to go. I know that 150 may not be a very low weight to many of my thinner friends (when I was young that would have been my super-fat weight!), but I need a weight I can feel confident about sticking to. At my age and with thyroid issues 'dogging' me, I need a weight I can diligently maintain and feel good about myself.

What would be a good weight for you, an honest weight, a weight you can hold to once you reach it? That's the goal to strive for, not the unrealistic goal you had when you were 20 years old.

The weight loss and calorie counting apps are so easy and amazing these days, and so are all the means of monitoring your exercise, such as the various fitness bracelets and the iWatch, which I have and use daily. They make it fun-ish!

In addition, take more time for your appearance, even when it's just dinner with your hubby. A good shower, a nice shampoo, and a set of decent clothes can go a long way toward making you feel not only human again, but also downright attractive, no matter your age.

Consider makeup part of your everyday routine rather than reserving it for that wedding once a year. Taking some pride in your appearance really does make a difference!

Since leaving Dogs Deserve Better, I've pledged to foster at least once a year, and—without the backing of an organization—rescued and fostered two dogs in November, finding them a great home together. These last diary entries will reflect my most-recent foster situation, and illustrate how you too can adapt to foster even when your circumstances change.

Foster Diary Background Update: I had to let my dog

Sloan go to the Rainbow Bridge in May—as he had come to the end of his road—and it never gets any easier. I rescued him from a Pennsylvania chain and fostered him, but grew so attached that I ended up adopting him myself.

He was past his prime by the time he was released from chains, and I knew he didn't have too many years left in him; he became my boy, and it was a great honor to love him and share my life and home with him for four years.

Sloan's last winter with me.

For the first time in 16 years, I found myself dogless. Dogless! It was both heaven and hell. Part of me loved it, loved the break from the constant training and 'mothering', but another part of me missed having a dog in my life. I felt confused.

My situation was now so different from when I wrote *Scream Like Banshee*. Two years after writing the book, I married my long-time Air Force friend, Joe Horvath; then, just a week later, moved the organization from my Pennsylvania home where I started Dogs Deserve Better to Michael Vick's former Bad Newz Kennels 15-acre property. I set about transforming a place of immense pain to a place of healing and love for chained dogs, calling it the Dogs Deserve Better Good Newz Rehab Center for Chained and Penned Dogs.

My husband went to Afghanistan for his work, while I lived on site at the center for almost three years, with as many as 14 dogs at any given time; I oversaw both the activist operations of the organization and the new addition of a DDB-owned rescue facility. It was exhausting!

I eventually hired a live-in manager, and was able to settle in the mountains of Northern Virginia with my husband Joe, Sloan, the occasional DDB foster dog, and our three cats.

Joe bought us a home in my dream location, situated on 35 acres overlooking a river, with a wooded stream and lots of wild critters and birds to fascinate me. I try to treasure each and every day, and memorize the beauty of the flowing water to take me through the upcoming retirement years when we'll most likely end up condo dwellers.

The downside of our property is that it's not very foster-dog friendly. Whereas my Pennsylvania home with two acres was easily amenable to doggie doors and fenced yards, this one is not so easy to fence as we sit atop a rocky slope leading down to the water.

Since Sloan was not a runner and was more inclined to lay on the front porch and keep watch over us, we just created a small potty yard with a doggie door in the back; that way if he needed to use the facilities when we were gone he could safely do so. The rest of the time we let him out the front door without concern about him leaving the property or bothering the neighbors...we can't see any from our house!

Sloan and I loved walking the trail along the stream, and as long as he was able, he'd run and explore the shallow waters, reveling in the freedom he'd never known all those years. I felt so blessed I could give him the gift of peace and happiness, because he deserved that and so much more.

So, in many ways I had 'completed' my part in the anti-chaining mission (if there is truly ever an end; I *had* gotten the issue off the ground, and provided the organization with a facility and 16 acres to build on). I was now dogless, and I was working through the emotional trauma of my last few years with the organization. I missed having a dog but loved the freedom I hadn't felt in so very long.

I took a few months to just breathe, to process, to grieve. To be. Who was I?

In August, Brynnan (my daughter who you'll remember I lost custody of during the Doogie trial) decided to move with me. Her father was fired from his job, and wanted her to re-locate with him to New Jersey. But by this point, at the age of 16 and having learned the truth of the situation, Brynnan refused. Her father could no longer control her actions, and so in the end she freed us both from his tyranny.

She moved to Northern Virginia with us, bringing her two cats to add to our three. We set about healing the damage our relationship had suffered, and I got a second chance at the daily mothering experience I'd missed out on for eight years. It's been wonderful.

By October, I was ready to foster a dog and fulfill the agreement I'd made with myself and the readers of *Scream Like Banshee*. I figured if all went well we could adopt the dog ourselves—but if the fit wasn't right, I'd find him/her a great home and rethink from there.

In November, the dog I wanted to rescue came to me.

Foster Diary: That face! That's the dog I want to foster! She's so beautiful, AND she's in Virginia, not too far from me. She was posted by a friend that I met while protesting another really bad case of animal abuse, so I send her a direct message asking for more information.

I feel the rescue excitement kicking in; for me there's a natural high that comes along with pulling a dog off a chain or out of a pen. I think that's why people get into hoarding situations, because they want that high, but then each additional animal is a burden and they become quickly overwhelmed. And the animals suffer.

The dog, Makayla (we would rename her Jewel, so I'll use that name from now on), looks like one of my first foster dogs, Sess, a long-haired shepherd mix who I adored. Of course I'm hoping I can keep her, but first I commit to fostering. Now that we have three opinions in the household, I have to take things a step at a time and see how they go.

She's living in a pen about an hour from me, and she has a daughter who's living inside the home who is also looking for rescue. I make arrangements for Brynnan and I to go meet the dogs the next day. I can't wait!

Chapter 26

HAPPINESS GOES AROUND: HOW YOU AFFECT THE DOGS

⅋

Four of the pups I had the pleasure of living with at the Good Newz Rehab Center for Chained and Penned Dogs. They ran twice a day in our 8-acre fenced field. That made for some happy dogs!

Truth: When you are happier your dogs are happier. Why? Because you don't yell as much, you don't whine as much, and you just may take 10 minutes to go throw the ball for your crazy foster. Oh, yeah, and they pick up on your energy.

Tip: Dog trainers agree, dogs follow our lead...when our energy is crazy, our dogs are crazier. Happiness makes you calmer, so stay in that place as much as and for as long as you possibly can. It will benefit every member of your household.

Repeat after me: Today I am happy, today I am calm. Today my pack is mellow too.

❧

I know how easy it is to slip into Scream-Like-Banshee mode, and have been known to partake myself on a few occasions, but it really does no one any good. There has to be a better way.

And there is. Making yourself happy is the key to that foundation, and not overwhelming yourself is crucial to that happiness. You decide your behavior in every circumstance; when I choose loving actions over angry reactions, I'm so relieved and pleased with myself that everyone in the household relaxes, sits back, and becomes happier by extension.

For me, the key to fostering is figuring out what triggers my stress buttons. Due to my less-than-stellar childhood, what I most hate is feeling abused or pushed around, especially by a man. That's why Banshee and I tended to butt heads on occasion—because he liked to push everyone around, and bam, there went my button!

But knowing what actions on his part—pushing past me was the big one—triggered my reactions, it was easier to calmly put into place a plan for containing his Banshee-itis Push-me-itis.

For instance, Banshee never got to walk through the door before me, unless I wasn't paying attention. Then he would push past me, and I'd grit my teeth and know that I let my vigilance slip; next time I would remember to make sure he was backed off before I got close to the door.

He also had to sit until he was relatively calm before he got his food dish. He was pretty much on the Nothing in Life is Free plan.

I knew he didn't mean to be crazy. He was a purebred Lab with an overabundance of energy, who was seriously in need of a job. He spent six years at the end of a chain without even a toy to chew on. How did he survive?

What are you trigger points? Figure out what engages your Scream-Like-Banshee-itis, and find a way to stop it before it's too late. Remember, being happy and calm benefits everyone in your household. Not just you, but the dogs and the kids and your hubby or wife will also appreciate it!

My new foster, Jewel, can't wait to get out of that pen.

Foster Diary: Brynnan and I make the hour drive over the Shenandoah Mountains to where the dogs live. When we hit Page County and travel through the countryside, I'm saddened to see how many dogs are living chained or penned here still. It's a beautiful land, but many of those who call it home are not enlightened in their care of animals.

Really, how hard is it to understand that a dog or cat deserves basic loving care and respect? It frustrates me! I'm a country girl at heart, but living in the country is always a challenge due to the mentality one consistently comes up against.

The sight that greets us upon arrival. Onyx, the black lab/chow cross is running loose with a little dog, while Jewel waits in her pen.

As I'm no longer with a rescue group, I have created my own surrender forms and transfer of ownership paperwork. I've learned how important it is by now to ensure when you rescue a dog from a chain or any other situation that you obtain proof that you do indeed 'own' the dog. (Although this isn't a term that you and I would put to spending our lives with a dog, it's the legal verbiage.) The last thing you need is to rescue a dog and then be accused of theft. Take it from me!

The man immediately lets Jewel out of the pen, along with a beagle who's living in the cage next to her. He has four dogs living there—two inside with him, and two outside in pens. His wife was disabled and he claims that she rescued all the dogs, but I choose not to get into any kind of verbal sparring with him as to why two of them are stuck outside. I just resolve to get them out of there, and I've learned you do indeed catch more flies with honey than vinegar.

As soon as he lets Jewel and the beagle loose, they run off up the hill and into the woods. Huh. Well, that didn't go as planned! Onyx runs with them too, but she quickly returns. She is very skittish with strangers, but loving with the man she considers her family.

I decide that I can and will indeed foster both Onyx and Jewel after he tells me they're good with cats, and I also ask about the beagle's future. I find out that he's willing to let her go too, but I can't take three into my home. Luckily I've taken some good photos of her in the pen, and I can use them to network to find her a foster home too.

Jewel finally returns about 1/2 hour later, during which time we were forced to make awkward small talk with the owner and try to get Onyx to come to us. He has no vet records for either of them, but says they are spayed, so I hope he's telling the truth. Without the backing of a nonprofit, all the vet care will be on me, unless I can convince some of my former supporters to chip in for the dogs.

Chained cats. Seriously. I shit you not. There were eight of them. I learned that shortly thereafter the owners allowed a local cat group to build them a big enclosure. At least it's better than a chain!

We finally get the dogs loaded up and we're on our way home. They are stinky and excited, and Jewel's back end is one big mat-fest. She's going to require a trip to the groomers to handle that mess! It's beyond my capabilities.

We're driving on twisty back roads when I spot a bunch of chained cats. Cats! Chained! Oh, my God, I'd seen this place on the internet! I turn around and go back to get a better look at the situation and some pics of the animals. There are both chained dogs and cats, I count about eight of each.

I park in a church lot about 1/8 mile up the road, and walk down the street with my camera. Unfortunately, I don't have my zoom so I don't get the best pics, as I'm not about to trespass. The owners had driven away, but as my luck would have it, they come back because they saw me slowing down to look at the cats.

While I'm taking pictures—from the road, clearly NOT trespassing or illegal in any way—they pull up next to me and tell me I'm trespassing. Um. I wasn't born yesterday, and am well-aware by this time of the laws regarding trespassing. So I get into an argument with them about their cats and the fact that my activities are perfectly legal.

She goes down to my car to get a look at my license place, and I take their photo as she drives away. Luckily for me, I had parked in such a way that my car camera videotaped my walk up the road and it's very clear that I never trespassed.

By the time I get home an hour later, a sheriff is waiting at my doorstep! I tell him I have video evidence that I didn't trespass, that they are guilty of animal abuse, and he gives me the number for the Page County sheriff to call.

I call the sheriff and tape the entire conversation with him. He admits that others have called repeatedly about the same situation, but claims his hands are tied according to the law. I tell him I have evidence that I didn't trespass, and he says it all depends on if the people try to press charges with the magistrate or not. He himself won't press charges.

I never get charged, but I prepare all my evidence just in case. It's so frustrating to be harassed by animal abusers, and have them never get in trouble themselves! These folks lie through their teeth. Always. Please take a ton of photos and video when you go on rescue missions, because sooner or later your evidence will be needed to protect yourself.

Chapter 27

YOUR HEALTH AND THEIRS: EXERCISING WITH THE DOGS

℘

Even though our dogs at the Good Newz Rehab Center could run offleash, I ensured that staff walked the field twice with each pack so that the dogs got lots of exercise (and so did the employees!). The dogs tend to hang around the staff members, so if the human is walking, so are the dogs. Staff usually took three pack walks both morning and evening.

Truth: A little exercise is exactly what the doctor ordered for both you and the dogs. By now I don't have to explain the reasons, right?

Tip: If you have an overwhelming number of dogs to walk, start slowly and find some volunteer help. Walk in shifts, different dogs on different days, or find your own workable solution. You will look better and feel better, and so will the dogs.

Repeat after me: I will walk the dogs at least three days a week, starting today.

⁂

Dogs really do need exercise. So do people. It only makes sense to put the two together, and kill two birds with one stone, right?

Admittedly, for the first four years of Dogs Deserve Better, there was little to no walking of the dogs who were fostered in my home. I had all kinds of excuses, i.e., the road is dangerous (it was!), I'm just too busy (I was!), there's too many dogs (there were!), and the list goes on and on.

Really, I just didn't make it a priority.

Banshee and The Beast enjoy a swim while on a walk in the woods.

Then we decided to make it a priority. I did some research, and began to truly understand the importance of the daily walk. Deb Carr, the former DDB Treasurer, walks her dogs almost every day, and she lectured me too, telling me I'd better get off my butt and get it in action because the dogs needed the exercise to burn off the excess energy.

I had been like so many people with a nice fenced yard, thinking the dogs got plenty of exercise just by going out in the yard everyday. But did they?

No! They never hung out in the yard, let alone undertook their own little health and fitness plan. Typically they would go out to do their business, check out everyone else's business, and then come back in, satisfied to be up my butt for the rest of the day.

Not enough exercise to make a hermit crab healthy and fit!

When I was still living in Pennsylvania, the town near us had created a Rails-to-Trails only about three miles from my house. My staff member and I got in the habit of loading the dogs up and driving the short distance to the trail for a walk. We loved it!

I also started taking them for long walks back in the deep woods, where they could run off leash and really get a good gallop in. It was amazing fun, until I had a couple scares—one involving a bear (he wasn't scared, I was!), and another involving a bobcat and a coyote. Between the wildlife who made those woods their home and the copious amounts of ticks I ended up pulling off the dogs each time we visited, I lost a bit of enthusiasm for the place. Shame, really...

Once I moved to Virginia to the Good Newz Rehab Center, we walked the dogs daily on leash around the 15-acre property until we finished the fencing, then they ran to their heart's content on daily pack walks. It was a pleasure to see.

For some winter fun, I used to walk with weights to music around the house, thinking the dogs would follow me and we'd have a mini-workout parade. Instead I'd end up in an obstacle course, those dogs who started to follow me quickly deciding to lay smack dab in the middle of the path, knowing they'd see me again on the next lap. I dodged akitas, labs, shepherds, and many a cat in my quest for a very simple 20 minute workout.

If you're one of those rescuers like I was who live in denial that the dogs (and you!) need exercise, I'm here to snap you out of it. They do. You do.

So what's the plan? Get on it today!

Foster Diary: Since I have a very small doggie yard at my new home, and a bear rudely lumbered over the 'tunnel' portion (smashing it to the ground), I have to leash walk Jewel and Onyx until they learn the property lines.

Admittedly, I've become spoiled and lazy since Sloan passed away in May. The cats can take care of their own bathroom needs, so I'm not used to getting up by 7:00 a.m. to handle pet care. And, unlike Sloan, Onyx and Jewel can't go outside without a human in tow.

Which all boils down to me, up at an ungodly hour, getting the girls out and walking them up the driveway. Exercise, schmexercise! It's cold outside, but probably not cold enough yet for the bears to be hibernating, so I'm hoping I don't have any nasty surprises waiting for me out there. I'm grumbly. I'm inconvenienced. Why did I do this again?

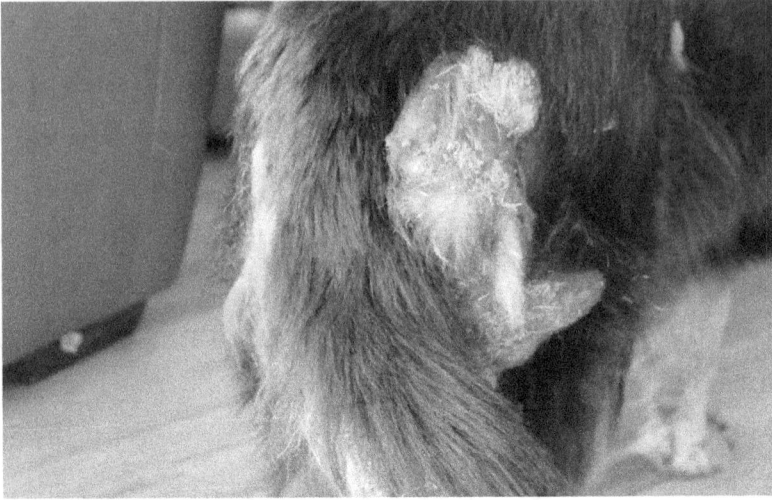

Jewel's back end and tail are totally matted.

At 8:00 a.m. I call the vet and then the groomer, and make appointments at both places for the girls, one today and one tomorrow. Thank Dog! I can only imagine the fleas and ticks and dirt a-roaming on these ladies. I'm so quick to forget how much work is involved in caring for rescue dogs!

The girls behave wonderfully at the vet's office, and it turns out they are both spayed, so I wasn't lied to for once. I still come away with a $450.00 bill for the bare necessities such as shots and testing. Jewel has Lyme disease and a bladder infection, and Onyx has Lyme disease and ehrlichiosis, another tick-born illness. They both are prescribed antibiotics.

That day I create a chip-in for their vet care, and ask my online friends if they'll throw in $10 or so to help get the girls back to health. Between all the food, leashes, vet care, and grooming, I'm looking at an initial output of $700 to get them in shape and ready for new homes! Yikes.

Did I mention I recommend fostering through an organization instead of on your own? Unless you have a ton of money, take it from me—it will be cost-prohibitive to rescue and rehab out of pocket.

Day One is full of activity, with only one minor potty accident on Jewel's part. Not too shabby! Fostering girl dogs... it's easier.

We are already running into trouble on the homefront, though. I really want to keep Jewel, but she's a runner, and I have to be able to trust my dog not to run off if I let her outside with me. Brynnan wants to keep Onyx, but Onyx is terrified of Joe, and barks nonstop when he comes home from work. We've got one strike for adopting each already, and it's only the first day. Let's see what Day Two holds.

The girls play well together, and really seem to enjoy each other's company. That makes me feel they should be adopted together if at all possible.

Chapter 28

LETTING GO: YOU ARE A STOP GAP

℘

Spotty was one of the dogs I lived with at the Good Newz Rehab Center. He slept in my room at night, and even went home with me at Christmas. He was a hard one to let go, but he moved on to the perfect home for him.

Truth: The day comes when we all have to let go of our foster dogs, even if it's death that do us part. Understand you are put in their life for a limited time to bring them love, health, and training, and then let them move along to their destiny.

Tip: Now that you are healthier in body and spirit, it will be that much easier for you to love and let go! So do it...love them...let them go.

Repeat after me: I love my foster dogs. I know I've done my best, trained them, healed them, and now I'm letting them go to a home that will make all their doggie dreams come true!

❧

Yes, I'm talking to YOU...you've got to let go! You don't want to be a hoarder, right? Because those are your two options when you foster...let them move along to new and hopefully loving homes, or keep piling them into your house because you don't trust anyone else enough to meet their needs. How many dogs can you safely and happily handle? Not that many.

I know it's hard. OK, it's not that hard for me anymore, but I appreciate that it's hard for you. I pack their little back-pack, put their 'no givey-backy' sticker on their butts, and send them along to their new home with a casual wave.

But, in all honesty, it took me awhile to learn to love and let go. It was a necessary skill for me to master, and it is for you too if you want to keep fostering dogs.

For a time I gave myself a very strict 'no-keepy' rule for my foster dogs, because I initially rescued a lot of old dogs that were so sweet and I just couldn't part with them. But then guess what? I had no room for other fosters!

So I had to make a rule for myself. I've gotten very good at loving them casually and lightly for the first couple of months while I get them vetted, trained, and ready for new homes. After that, I—admittedly and against my better judgment—often become too attached as well.

At that point, no matter how insane they are (Magnum), or how wild they are (Banshee), they've weaseled their way into my heart and I love 'em. Just can't help it.

But I still let them go when it's time if a good home comes up. I make myself do it.

Delilah was a blind foster who we got off chains while still in Pennsylvania. She was a total sweetheart and my daughter Brynnan wanted to keep her, but over time it became apparent she would do better elsewhere. She was overly obsessed with the cats, and would stalk them relentlessly. I couldn't get her to stop. I finally decided to let her go, and she went to live with an woman who took her everywhere with her and spoiled her rotten. She traded up.

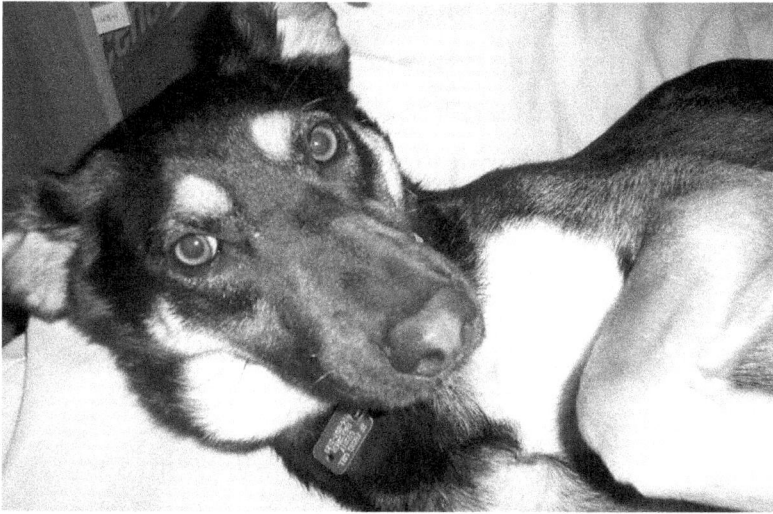

Delilah had always slept on my right side in bed at night, in the exact same spot, every single night. She turned her little belly up for me and Brynnan to rub, and she'd just lay there in doggie heaven while we caressed her soft skin. We both missed that. I still think of her every time I hear "Hey There Delilah"—we named her for that song—but I know it was for the best.

Remember these words of advice as your sweet old guys pass...don't keep the next one! Foster 'em, but let them go to a loving home. You will have more end-result happiness and more time for you.

Foster Diary: What, is it 7:00 a.m. already? Ugh. How long must this fostering go on! Haha. Seriously, though! I really got spoiled after Sloan passed away, and spent way too many mornings lounging in bed.

I get up to take the girls out for their morning walk up the lane, and I'm shivering in the cold. I do have to admit, though, once it's all said and done, I feel awake and alive from the fresh morning air and getting the blood flowing. I go bold and take Onyx off the leash halfway up the hill, and she does great with running but staying where I can keep my eye on her.

Jewel is pulling on the leash and crazy with wanting to run, too, though, but I just can't trust her. She doesn't know the area well enough yet, and she already has running in her blood from her life in the pen.

Shortly after breakfast I load them back into the car and drive them to the groomers for their 10:00 a.m. appointments. They will need to do quite a bit of shaving, on Jewel especially, but both girls have mats and long hair. I do some shopping and take a long walk and treat myself to lunch while I wait for them in town.

Gorgeous Jewel after the groomers. No more mats!

I'm thankful for my former wonderful DDB supporters and

friends who have chipped in to help me care for the girls, as I quickly raise $400.00 towards their care. That only leaves me $300 out of pocket, which is a lot more doable than the $700.00 I thought I'd have! I breathe a sigh of relief.

On Day Two, though, the challenges of fostering in my new environment mount. Jewel is too interested in the cats for Brynnan's comfort, and when the two girls 'pack up' they are starting to chase the cats, leading to turmoil and stress for the whole family.

Joe has said he'll help me build a new tunnel out of wood from the doggie door across the cement to the dog yard (about 4 feet), but we can't do that until his next break from work. That means I must continue to leash walk them or trust them off leash, and I'm not prepared to do that with Jewel yet.

My feral cat, Bootsie, is so traumatized that she won't leave the cat room at all, and is just cowering in fear all day and all night. Argh. I have made so much progress with her, and I feel like all my hard work is going down the tubes.

Between Onyx barking at Joe and Jewel targeting the cats, I'm feeling incredibly anxious, which isn't helping the situation at all. I make the decision to make no decisions one way or the other for three weeks, to see if it gets better or worse for the whole family. By the end of this period, the dogs will be trained and ready to be put up for adoption, and I will have a better idea if we can make this work on a family level. I'm not feeling optimistic at this point.

Chapter 29

MOVING ON: DOING IT ALL AGAIN, BUT WISER THIS TIME

⚬

Sampson was one of the last dogs I freed from the chain as part of Dogs Deserve Better. He will always hold a special place in my heart.

Truth: Fostering is one of the hardest commitments you will ever make to dogs in need. But it's also one of the most rewarding. Realize you CAN foster in a way that is not overwhelming to all and creates an end-result which is second to none.

Tip: Learn from your mistakes and keep on truckin'. There are no cut and dried, right and wrong answers to the challenge of fostering dogs, but continue to evolve and get smarter with each new foster.

Repeat after me: I've succeeded in bringing happiness not only to my foster dogs but to myself as well. I am now able to commit to fostering dogs in a way that nurtures all of us, knowing my own needs are acknowledged and met.

❧

I promise, if you take the tips in this book to heart, you will start to see changes in your life. Changes that are well-deserved and needed in order for you to be happy.

Don't stop fostering, but don't put your own needs on the back burner, never to be heard from again. You are important, and so are your innermost dreams and desires.

Get them out, dust them off, and indulge in them. The dogs will love you more, and you will love them more too.

Foster Diary: It's December 1st, and Jewel and Onyx have been in foster care with me for three weeks, the deadline I've given myself to decide whether we will adopt as a family or not.

I wish I could say things have improved, but there has been too much turmoil and stress with both of them here, and we cannot agree as a family on which one to adopt. I personally feel they deserve a home together, because they get along really well, and I'd love them to keep that bond.

Jewel has run into the woods almost every time I trusted her off leash, although she has come back shortly thereafter. It makes me incredibly stressed and nervous that she is getting herself into trouble out in the woods, and I wouldn't know where to find her to help her if she didn't come back. I adore her little face, and I love to hug on her. I could just squeeze her to pieces! She's a wonderful dog, but I'm not convinced she'd the right dog for us.

Bootsie the feral kitty and Brynnan are in agreement on that. Joe likes her and could be persuaded to keep her, but he does acknowledge that the running off is a problem.

Onyx cannot get over her fear of Joe. He works long days, and is often gone from the house for 15 hours at a time. He gets home, only to grab some sleep and get back on the road to work again. He has neither the time nor the inclination to try to win her heart on the long days of work, and on his off days he wants to do something fun or get some chores done. Their situation is stressful and anxiety-inducing, and the happiness level of our home has taken a serious nosedive.

As a family we decide to put them both up for adoption, citing that we'd prefer they get a home together. If that doesn't happen, but we find the perfect home for one of the girls, we will see how we do with the other and rethink from there.

I readily admit that fostering dogs was easier when democratic votes didn't need to be taken of all family members at each step along the way! There's something to be said for good old-fashioned autocracy. Ha!

Chapter 30

SEEKING HELP: KNOWING WHEN TO CALL IN THE CAVALRY

☙

Onyx after her trip to the groomer. I realized, because she was a black chow mix like the dog who attacked me, some of my anxiety in fostering her was due to that trauma, so I've been working on it in therapy.

Truth: Sometimes as a result of fostering you encounter a trauma that is beyond the scope of self-healing, or you don't know where to start. Professional help is an option for everyone in times of serious trouble. Compassion Fatigue is a very real danger for those of us in animal rescue fields, and requires immediate self-care and often professional help.

Tip: Fostering dogs often comes with psychologically disturbing events, such as arrests, dog attacks on a person or other dog, or devastating illness. Reach out to a therapist or spiritual advisor for help when needed.

Repeat after me: If my trauma is too great, I pledge to know when to get help and take my mental health seriously. I will reach out to a local support system when needed. I matter!

❧

I hope no other foster parent in the history of the world suffers the amount of trauma that I have as a result of my rescue work, but it would be wishful thinking to expect you too couldn't or wouldn't fall victim to Compassion Fatigue Syndrome or Post Traumatic Stress Disorder.

When I was still in Pennsylvania I suffered three colossally damaging events, as well as lesser events that 'piled on'. I was arrested for helping Doogie and criminalized for my stand against his abuse; I lost my daughter during the trial for him; and I was attacked by one of my foster dogs.

I should have gone for professional help during that period, but I didn't, suffering depression and anxiety as a result. I tried to handle my feelings on my own, to power through, and I thought I'd done an ok job of it. In hindsight, I wish I'd made my mental health more important than I did.

I don't want you to make the same mistake.

Just what is Compassion Fatigue Syndrome, anyway? In a nutshell, it is caused by the pain of witnessing or bearing repeated trauma while caring for others (in our case, animals) and putting the care of others before ourselves. We see no end to the need and no way to make it stop. The resulting apathy, detachment, inability to express emotions, and substance abuse head a long list of manifestations now associated with and labeled as Compassion Fatigue Syndrome.

I now believe that when I moved the organization to Michael Vick's former fight compound in Virginia, I was already suffering from Compassion Fatigue Syndrome. When we arrived there, it was me, one other employee, and eight dogs. We had no money, no fencing, a facility mortgage, and people expecting us to be up and running a full shelter the second we walked through the door.

The pressure was enormous. On top of that, the locals that I naively thought would welcome us and be happy we were transforming Vick's compound organized against us, trying to force us out of the community.

It appeared they would rather have a dogfighting ring in their county than a dog rescue organization. I learned all too well why Vick had chosen Surry County to begin with...he was welcome there. We were not.

Everywhere I turned there was hatred directed toward Dogs Deserve Better and me in particular, and I was suffering from a monstrous depression I could not find my way clear of. I thought I went to Virginia to do something good, but instead I was vilified at every turn.

Then a trauma I could never have imagined befell me. I

had an employee who was embezzling from the organization, padding her paychecks, and to add insult to injury, not bothering to show up for work at least once a week. In an organization with three or four employees, every employee is crucial to the team and must pull his/her weight. By the time I realized the employee was embezzling and filed an investigation with the state police, she had already 'gotten in bed' with Vick's buddy and Commonwealth Attorney Gerald Poindexter to frame me for animal cruelty.

I came home from a ten-day honeymoon trip to St. Lucia with my husband to an arrest for a very 'nonspecific' animal cruelty charge, and no details were ever given to me. I had no idea what I had supposedly done!

Can you imagine being arrested and officers refusing to even tell you what you were being arrested for? The truth was they didn't tell me because they didn't know themselves. They had nothing but a goal to destroy my reputation.

I was beyond freaked out and didn't know what was going on; it took me a week to piece together what had happened to me. News vans, called by Poindexter and his animal control officer Tracy Terry, sat outside our facility waiting for my arrest to ensure it was publicized nationwide.

My reputation and what little remained of my self-esteem were destroyed in one fell swoop. Well-played, Surry County. They wanted rid of us, and they were making damn sure it happened, one way or another.

Luckily, I was smart enough to have a staff member photograph the entire arrest. The camera was on the wrong setting, but she got enough photos and evidence of their false charges against me to save my ass when we got to court.

They were so stupid that they seized a dog who looked beautiful, a perfectly healthy pitbull named Jada. If we hadn't taken pictures, they might have succeeded in their effort to destroy me/DDB, but we brought the photos to court along with a vet to testify in my defense.

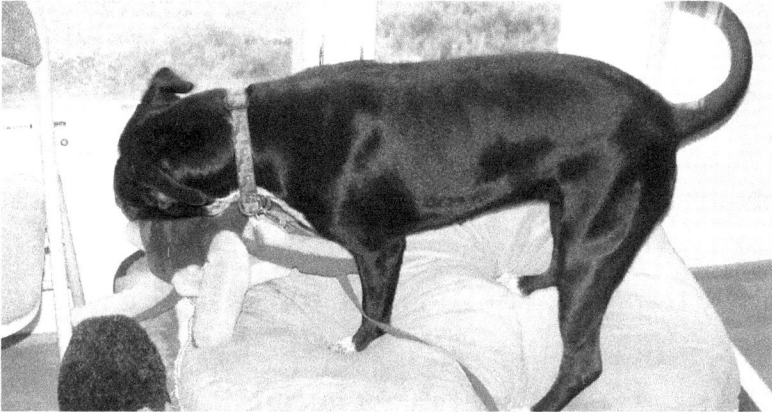

Jada pictured playing with her toys while waiting to be seized. Even in black and white you can see how muscular she was and how shiny her fur was. The dog was in beautiful shape.

On the day of my arrest I just wanted to die. I felt such shame and guilt for something I hadn't done, but knew everyone else believed I had. I was devastated. And that was exactly what they wanted: they wanted to destroy me and Dogs Deserve Better, and if it took a frame job and a conspiracy of liars to accomplish that, so be it.

When the police left, I let all the media into the center, but I was told by my attorney not to speak to them. I had staff take them to every room, show them every dog, into every area of our facility, and out into the dog yards. That night on the news they ran the explosive story of my arrest, but played it overtop of pictures of beautiful, healthy, and happy dogs. They even showed Jada getting into the animal control vehicle, looking muscular and shiny, and certainly far from abused. I could only hope the video created doubts in the minds of viewers.

We had nothing to hide. I had done nothing wrong.

I cried for two days straight, and I knew if I didn't get some psychological help I was going to be in real trouble. I started seeing a therapist immediately, and for the first month I just sat in her office and cried for an hour. She helped me through the worst time of my life, and I hope if you ever get into a similarly traumatic situation, you too recognize when you're in trouble and get the help you need.

We kicked Surry County's ass in court, not once but three times, winning a nondisclosed financial settlement for myself and Dogs Deserve Better for what they'd done to destroy us. We settled for much less than we deserved, because I didn't have the money to fight any longer; I had to take the symbolic victory and call it a day. But, at least we won!

In the words of the judge, which made VERY clear his opinion on whether any abuse occurred: "There's an old expression, a picture is worth a thousand words, and I'm looking at the pictures of November 6, 2011. [The day Jada was rescued by DDB.] This dog was in rough shape. I see scars, pretty bad scars all over the forehead, if you will, then those underneath the back—I guess that's left leg. Bad scar up under the body on the upper part of the leg. You see scars on her rump, or rear end if you will. These are pretty nasty scars. You said she may have been thrown out of a truck; I don't know. But then I'm looking at pictures, I guess that's about 10 or 11 months later, on August 27th—that looks like a very healthy dog to me.

"I've unfortunately been involved in a lot of dog cases and I've seen a lot of pictures. Quite frankly you see the picture and that's the end of it. Count the ribs, scars all over, malnutrition. I'm sure you have, too.

"Yet this dog—and everybody agrees these pictures are accurate. They're presented as evidence. Nobody's disputed them. And all the scars are gone. This dog looks like it's done an amazing job of being healed. I looked at this full frontal face and I can't find any evidence that these scars that were there just 10 months before, if I didn't know that they had been there before, I wouldn't see it.

"So the veterinarian—and I'm sure she's a sworn professional, sworn in under oath, professional person. I can't—I've had very few vets in my life that didn't love animals, or they never would have been a vet in the first place. It's almost impossible to be a veterinarian without loving animals. That's almost what always draws them. And I feel comfortable that the doctor would have said no, the dog's being treated terribly, and in all my cases before they've always been a witness for the Commonwealth.

"In this case I just see pretty strong evidence—or let me just say this, a VERY CLEAR LACK OF EVIDENCE that this dog has been cruelly treated. So I'm going to deny the petition. And of course I think the disposition once I do that is order that the dog be returned to the rightful owner."

You have no idea how grateful I was that the judge wasn't in Surry County's pocket! I was terrified that he would be, and that no matter what evidence we presented, it wouldn't be enough. But in this case, justice was finally served, and Surry County corrupt officials were shown the door.

I pray nothing similar ever happens to you! No one with a good heart deserves the torture I went through at the hands of Surry County and an embezzling employee (who they refused to charge—of course—despite considerable evidence against her, all compiled by the Virginia State Police special officer for embezzling. Didn't matter.)

By 2015, I had nothing left to give to Dogs Deserve Better. I stepped down from the organization, and put myself back into counseling for PTSD to deal with all I'd gone through. I just couldn't get past the pain of it all. I'm still in therapy now, but have come a long way in healing the grief and the trauma that overwhelmed my very soul.

I would never in a million years have thought I'd suffer so much because of my desire to help chained and penned dogs. I was merely a human seeking my mission in the world, a way to make a difference. Instead I became a punching bag for abusers and the corrupt officials who protect them.

If you're fostering dogs, I'm sure that you are just trying to make a difference too; you don't deserve to be traumatized for it, and I hope you never are. If you do get into a bad situation, please, feel no shame about seeking professional help. You're a stronger person if you can admit that you need aid rather than living in denial and possibly falling off the edge.

The people who love you want you to stick around. Get

the help you need when you need it.

Remember, you can take it slowly. You can foster one dog at a time, for an organization near you, and they will cover all vet care costs and often handle the adoptions, too. All you do is provide the love and training that the dog needs, and then let him/her go to what is hopefully a loving and forever home.

I thank you all for opening your homes and your hearts to a dog in need. You have my gratitude. I hope this book can help bring you peace in a hectic world, and make your fostering experience better, for both you and the dogs.

The girls swimming together in the river.

Foster Diary: Well, I did it! I found an adopter who wants both girls; they live on ten acres near Richmond, Virginia, and have recently lost two dogs to old age. When I meet the family, they immediately plop down on the floor with the dogs, and proceed to love them up the entire time we discuss their adoption. The mom works as an artist in an at-home studio, so the dogs will have company virtually 24/7. There are no cats in the family as they are allergic, so there's no worry about kitties, and they have a stream on the property for the dogs to romp and play in. I'm ecstatic for them!

We go over all the challenges they will face, and they are well-armed with all necessary vet care paperwork and signed adoption and transfer of ownership forms.

I'm lamenting the loss of Jewel, and Brynnan is decrying the loss of Onyx. But we know they are happy, and together, and in the right home for them. The ending was the best for everyone involved.

And the right dog for our home? We applied to foster a sweet shepherd/collie cross we saw online, and found our new family member! I continue to commit to fostering and making a difference for dogs in need...one dog at a time! Who's next?

Me with Jewel, the week before her adoption.

AFTERWORD

ॐ

I know that last chapter is a heavy read, but believe me, it was even harder to live through! For a long time after the smear campaign I felt so ashamed, and so guilty like I'd really done something wrong when I didn't.

I hesitated to rework *Scream Like Banshee* into this second edition, because I thought "who am I to talk to you about fostering, when I was arrested for animal cruelty?" But the truth of the matter is that my arrest—because it was so obviously false—makes me the BEST person to talk to you about the risks we undertake in rescue. Forewarned is forearmed.

Rescuers and activists are not wanted in counties where animal abuse is rampant. You can be sure authorities are participating in the abuse or covering for those who are. They don't like animal rescuers pointing out their deficiencies, and they will often stop at nothing to destroy them. My case is clear evidence of the depths to which they will stoop. Always, always, always take pictures of everything authorities do when it involves you and your safety. Please protect yourself.

P.S. Want to know what happened with Banshee? He never did get a home, but he loved me and thought I was his mom. And of course I was; I miss him. If you want to watch the video of his Last Fetch, you can view it here: http://bit.ly/1YPo6dg.

Acknowledgments

$\mathcal{G}$

Thanks first and foremost to my husband Joe and my children, Rayne and Bryn, for standing by my side no matter what has come our way. You've been proud of me, and you've loved me in spite of the world's attempts to bring me down. I love you greatly. I hope to always support you in whatever you choose to do with this life.

I'd also like to thank my friends and DDB supporters in the animal rights and animal rescue movements who've stuck by me even when Surry County was doing their worst to destroy me. So many saw through the lies, and for those who did, I'm grateful.

To the vet who stood in the courtroom with me, Dr. Leslie Dragon, I can never repay you for the kindness you showed to me and to Dogs Deserve Better. You are a vet for all the right reasons, and your mobile veterinary services were a blessing to us.

I'm working on a book about the purchase of Vick's Bad Newz Kennels, and there will be many more folks who assisted me to thank in those pages, as well as some scary villains to out. I hope you'll join me next year when that book's released!

About the Author

Tamira Ci Thayne is the pioneer of the anti-chaining movement in America, and founder and former CEO of Dogs Deserve Better, a nonprofit working exclusively for chained and penned dogs.

Tamira holds a Doctorate of Naturology from the American Institute of Holistic Theology, and is an ordained interfaith minister through the same theological college.

She's trying her hand at vegan baking—taking failure to a whole new level—and bears a love for kayaking the river in a decidedly amateurish fashion. She adores her human and fur family, and also all the wild critters she secretly names. She has a sneaking suspicion that the critters don't share the same fondness for her.

Tamira is the author of *Scream Like Banshee* and *Capitol in Chains*, and editor of *Unchain My Heart* and *A New Name for Worthless*. She is the illustrator and editor of *Puddles on the Floor*.

She recently founded Who Chains You: Publishing and Spiritual Mentoring for Animal Activists and Rescuers, with *Foster Doggie Insanity* being the first book carried under the new publisher. Learn more at whochainsyou.com.

ALSO BY TAMIRA THAYNE

Tamira Thayne

The WRATH of DOG

The Chained Gods Series Book 1

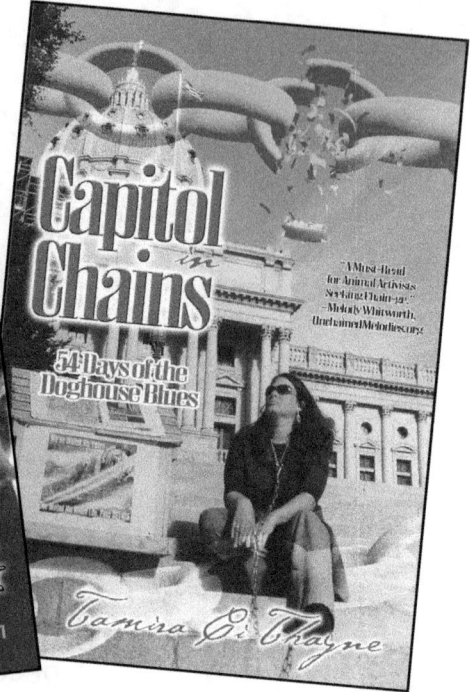

Capitol in Chains

54 Days of the Doghouse Blues

"A Must-Read for Animal Activists Seeking Chain-ge."
-Melody Whitworth, UnchainedMelodies.org

Tamira C. Thayne

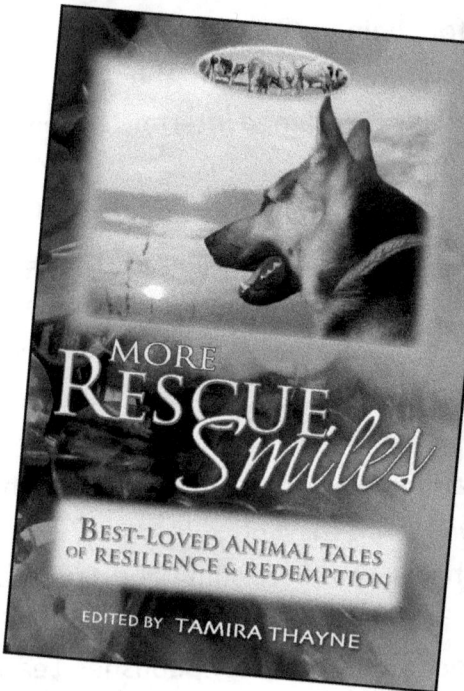

MORE RESCUE Smiles

BEST-LOVED ANIMAL TALES
OF RESILIENCE & REDEMPTION

EDITED BY TAMIRA THAYNE

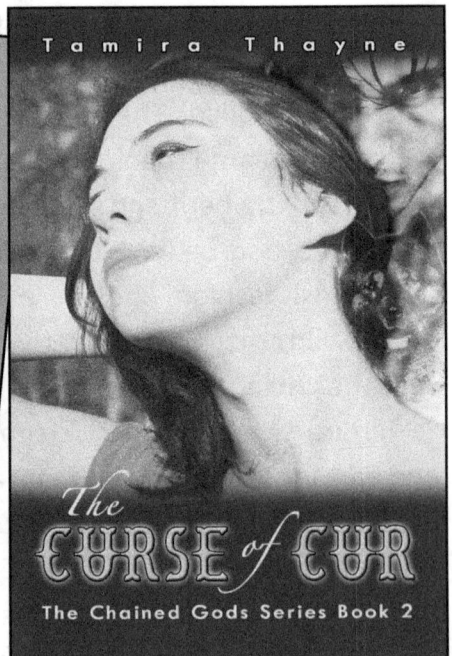

Tamira Thayne

The CURSE of CUR

The Chained Gods Series Book 2

ALSO BY TAMIRA THAYNE

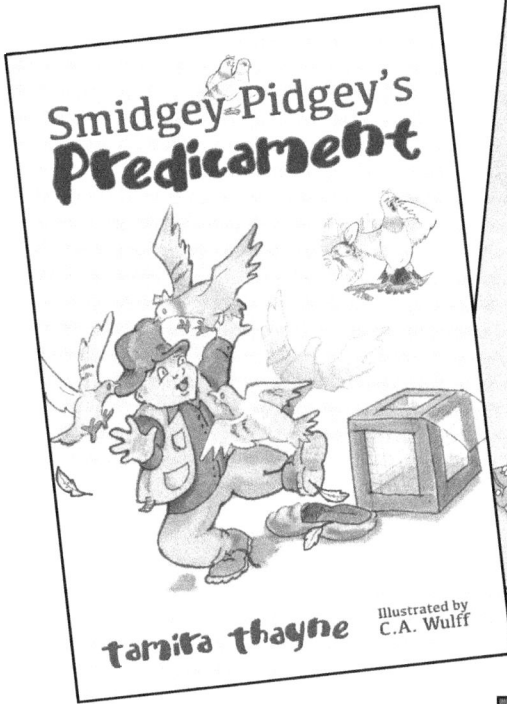

Smidgey-Pidgey's **Predicament**

tamira thayne Illustrated by C.A. Wulff

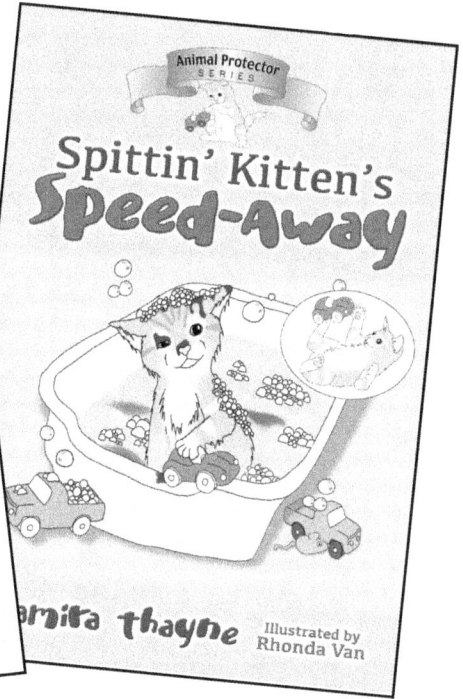

Animal Protector SERIES

Spittin' Kitten's **Speed-Away**

tamira thayne Illustrated by Rhonda Van

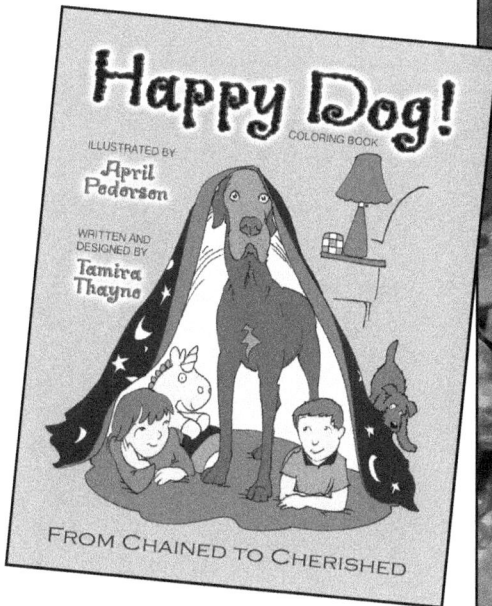

Happy Dog! COLORING BOOK

ILLUSTRATED BY **April Pederson**

WRITTEN AND DESIGNED BY **Tamira Thayne**

FROM CHAINED TO CHERISHED

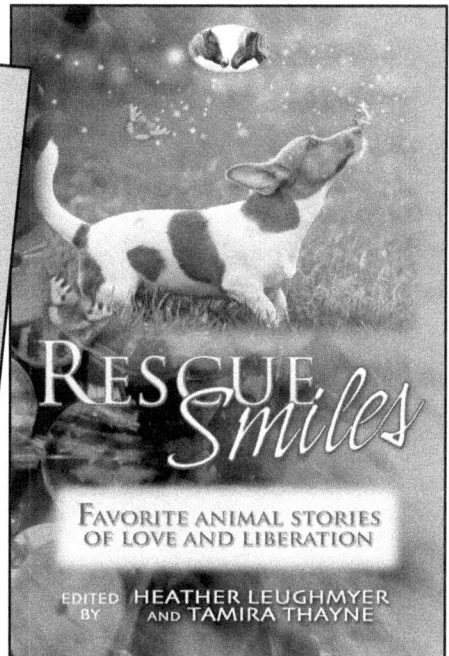

RESCUE Smiles

FAVORITE ANIMAL STORIES OF LOVE AND LIBERATION

EDITED BY HEATHER LEUGHMYER AND TAMIRA THAYNE

* 9 7 8 0 9 8 4 2 8 9 7 8 3 *